TOWARD A WORKING PHILOSOPHY

OF ADULT EDUCATION

by

Jerold W. Apps

Professor, Department of Agricultural and Extension Education
University of Wisconsin

May, 1973

Syracuse University

PUBLICATIONS IN CONTINUING EDUCATION
and
ERIC CLEARINGHOUSE ON ADULT EDUCATION

CBPac

OCCASIONAL PAPERS

A special series devoted to documents which, though prepared in a specific context and for a limited audience, are judged to be of such general interest that they merit wider distribution than that for which they were originally intended. They are presented in the hope that they will contribute to the more general sharing of information and opinion about questions of importance in the field of adult education.

This Occasional Paper may be secured for $3.00 per copy by writing to:

Publications in Continuing Education
Svracuse University
Syracuse, N.Y. 13210

For information about standing orders, please write to the above address.

LIBRARY OF CONGRESS CATALOGUE CARD:

ISBN NUMBER: 0-87060-059-1

Syracuse University
PUBLICATIONS IN CONTINUING EDUCATION
and
ERIC CLEARINGHOUSE ON ADULT EDUCATION

PREFACE

Every profession must eventually grapple with a working philosophy. Adult education, considered still an emerging field of professionalization by man, has not fully developed an acceptable working philosophy.

To help adult educators in their pursuit of a working philosophy, the ERIC Clearinghouse on Adult Education invited Dr. Jerold W. Apps to prepare a monograph on the topic. This publication represents his response.

In this publication, Apps has put adult education into the context of current educational philosophies. He has succeeded in presenting some highly complex philosophical systems in language easy to understand by the practitioner, mainly because of his familiarity with and use of numerous examples.

Adult educators are indebted to Jerold Apps for his scholarship in the preparation of this monograph. Members of the profession are invited to offer suggestions for the improvement of the review.

Thanks are also due to Bea Marcks for typing the manuscript and to Doris Chertow and the Syracuse University Publications in Continuing Education for making this monograph available more widely.

Stanley M. Grabowski
Director
ERIC Clearinghouse on Adult Education

ACKNOWLEDGMENTS

Raghbir Singh and Roger Williams, graduate students in Extension Education at the University of Wisconsin, were of great help in critically reviewing this manuscript in its early drafts.

Graduate students enrolled in my seminars for the past three years contributed many of the ideas in this monograph, and were responsible for the clarification of much of my thinking in this area.

Nancy Trager has my gratitude for typing the various drafts of the manuscript.

Jerold W. Apps
Professor
University of Wisconsin

TABLE OF CONTENTS

Chapter 1

INTRODUCTION

> As things are . . . mankind (is) by no means agreed
> about the things to be taught, whether we look to
> virtue or the best life. Neither is it clear whether
> education is more concerned with intellectual or
> moral virtue. The existing practice is perplexing: no
> one knowing on what principle we should proceed--
> should the useful in life, or should virtue, or should
> the higher knowledge be the aim of our training; all
> three opinions have been entertained. Again about
> the means there is no agreement: for different per-
> sons, starting with different ideas about the nature
> of virtue, naturally disagree about the practice of it. [1]

This could have been written by a contemporary adult educator concerned with a problem facing most adult educators--not ". . . knowing
on what principle we should proceed . . ." But the problem isn't unique
to our age, for the above was written 2,500 years ago by Aristotle as
he described the problems educators confronted in ancient Greece.

Hundreds of questions face adult educators each day. Some we can
answer with confidence; others we answer, but with less confidence,
and still others often go unanswered.

This monograph is concerned with developing a personal working
philosophy of adult education as a step toward ". . . knowing on what
principle we should proceed." Developing a working philosophy is the
search for principles--the discovery and development of what we believe
about various basic elements of adult education.

Some people argue that we all have working philosophies of adult
education. That is essentially true, but a working philosophy is on a
continuum with common sense on one end, and ultimate working philosophy
on the other.

Common sense   Ultimate working philosophy

|---|

A working philosophy is never completely developed, the ultimate
working philosophy never reached. We're always moving toward, hope-
fully, a more complete, and thus more useful, working philosophy. We
all have a liberal allowance of common sense acquired through years of
living. Common sense allows us to make day-to-day decisions about the
educational problems we face in whatever our adult education positions
might be. But as Brubacher says,

> . . . common sense as a homespun philosophy of education
> is often adequate to make immediate resolutions of

conflicting demands on the teacher's attention, but it easily breaks down if the severe strain is placed on it of formulating long-range educational policies.[2]

Also, common sense responses often vacillate from one situation to another, and from one time to another. Common sense, though it may help us get by in the short run, doesn't give us the basic set of principles we often need to deal with the broader and often more long-range problems.

The development of a working philosophy of adult education starts with common sense. Our concern is to refine it, and move it along the continuum to the right. We refine our common sense (develop our working philosophy) in two basic ways--scientifically and philosophically.

Following the scientific approach we select a specific educational problem, define the variables as carefully and precisely as we can, and then try to determine the relationship of the variables to one another. We strive to get specific answers to specific questions. Insofar as possible, the entire process is rigidly controlled to prevent outside variables from influencing the results of our research.

The philosophic method of extending and refining common sense moves in quite a different direction from the scientific one. It aims not at a solution of just a limited number of factors and variables which inhere in an educational problem and which can be rigidly controlled experimentally, but at one which includes every factor or variable which is either directly or remotely relevant to the problem.[3]

Looking at educational problems from a philosophic point of view becomes exceedingly complex, often frustrating, and always open-ended. To look at problems philosophically, we draw together information from many sources, including common sense and tradition. We include information from the life sciences of biology and psychology; from the social sciences of sociology, political science, economics; and information from educational history, religion, and morals.[4]

In taking advantage of all these data, however, one should note that philosophy itself uncovers no new facts. It processes the facts of other disciplines but owns none of its own.[5]

This monograph, then, focuses on the development of a personal working philosophy of adult education, with more emphasis on the philosophical approach than on the scientific approach. This in no sense is to downgrade the significance of the scientific approach to refining common sense. As it has been in the past, and will continue to be in the future, the search for answers to educational problems scientifically must continue. Along with the scientific search, and often occurring at the same time-- a hand-to-hand working relationship--should be the broader look at problems suggested in the philosophical approach.

The Need for a Working Philosophy

As a preface to discussion of how we might further develop a working philosophy of adult education, let's look briefly at some reasons why a working philosophy can be of practical use to adult educators.

There are several reasons. They are presented on the following list which, however, is not all-inclusive.

1. Within the field of adult education a need exists to consider three kinds of questions when determining future programming: "what is" questions, "why it is" questions, and "what should be" questions.

"What is" questions continue the basis for assessing current programs or determining what's happening now in the way of programming.

"Why it is" questions seek a deeper probing into programming with an attempt to analyze why a particular program is being conducted. Both the "why it is" and the "what is" can be answered following the scientific approach. The "what should be," applied to future programs, is a philosophical question.

Adult educators often find it easier to deal with the "what is" and the "why it is" inquiries as a basis for programming. The "what should be" problems are often more difficult. Of course, a close relationship to one another exists among the three types of questions. To deal with the "what should be," it's usually helpful to have a clear understanding of what now is happening and why it is happening. Based on that information, and additional information that comes from looking at situations broadly, the adult educator makes some decisions about future programming.

A working philosophy can help the adult educator deal with "what should be" questions. If we believe, for example, that the overall purpose of the adult educator is to help people become more self-actualized, we then make decisions about future programming that are in accord with that belief.

A well-developed working philosophy can also help the adult educator in his analysis of "what is" and "why it is" situations. The adult educator will search for the underlying assumptions of current programs and then constantly relate them to his beliefs about adult education. He'll also, in his analysis, be more conscious of contradictions in assumptions that may be evident in some programs now being conducted. He'll want to know if decisions about programs or choices among programs are made based on carefully considered assumptions, or if choices are made because of tradition, expediency, or some adult educator's notion about what he thought might work. This analysis would continue as additional suppositions are identified and examined.

For example, let's assume there's serious water pollution in a given community, and that an adult education program is being developed to

3

deal with the problem. What are examples of beliefs that should be examined? They may include presumptions such as these:

   a. An adult education program can contribute to solving the water pollution problem. There may be problems that are primarily political, and adult education can make little contribution to their solution. Do we believe that an adult education program can make a contribution to a community water pollution problem?
   b. People in the community want to solve the water pollution problem. If we can't accept that assumption, an adult educational program will have little impact.

Finally, the adult educator with a well-developed working philosophy will more easily discover "why it is" and "what should be" questions as he thinks and acts on program decisions.

   2. The individual adult educator often feels so small a part of a large agency that he looks to that agency for all of his direction.

David Riesman[6] suggests there are many "other-directed men" who prefer to follow others than themselves, not because they necessarily believe in those they follow, but because the security forces are greater when they do.

Without a well-defined personal working philosophy of adult education, it's easy to see how the adult educator could become trapped into blindly following the direction of his agency or institution. A working philosophy can help him see how what he believes relates to what he perceives is the direction of his agency. And further, rather than taking all direction from his agency, the adult educator should be influencing the direction his agency is taking. Without a well-formulated working philosophy, such leadership is difficult if not impossible.

   3. The adult educator needs a foundation for looking at the relationship of educational problems.

Many educational problems are considered often in isolation from one another. To adequately solve one problem may adversely affect another situation, indeed create another problem. A simple example: An enlightened vice-president of a large corporation, a firm believer in adult education, seeks to solve the problem of a junior executive with narrow background, by encouraging him to take courses in the liberal arts. This liberal education, however, succeeds in creating a new problem: the young man becomes so discontent in his new perception of his job that he quits to seek more satisfying employment.

A well-developed working philosophy can provide the educator with an attitude that requires all of the pieces in the educational situation to be considered, not only where there's a problem.

   4. The adult educator needs to see the relationship of adult education activities to society.

4

For many years adult education has been criticized as a marginal activity. It is criticized as marginal in two ways: (a) by not being institutionalized as such, "Usually it has been a peripheral function of an institution whose main business was something else, as evening schools for adults are incidental to a school system organized to serve children and youth, or as extension is to a university, "[7] and (b) by conducting activities that are seen by many people as non-important or at best fringe to the major concerns of society. Referred to are classes in hat making, cake decorating, and the like.

Many have suggested, and indeed a growing number of people are insisting, that adult education deal with the problems faced by individuals, by communities, and by the larger society.

A well thought out working philosophy can be the foundation for helping to institutionalize adult education activities, when such institutionalization is necessary to give visibility to adult education and to help it acquire necessary resources.

Similarly, a working philosophy can be the basis for relating adult education activities to the important problems of individuals and societies, and in more than simply a token kind of way.

5. A well-developed working philosophy can provide the adult educator with an approach for dealing with such long standing and basic questions as:

   a. What is reality; how do we know what is real?
   b. What is of value in society?
   c. What is the nature of man?
   d. How is knowledge acquired?
   e. What is education?
   f. What is the purpose of education?

   Within adult education there are such questions as:

   a. What is adult education?
   b. What is the purpose of adult education?
   c. What is the role of adult education in society?

6. In a broader, personal sense, development of a working philosophy can provide a deeper meaning to the adult educator's life.

As Royce says, "The key to personal meaning lies in the structure of each individual's epistemological and value hierarchies. "[8] What we believe about how knowledge is obtained, and what we believe about what's of value serves as the foundation for personal meaning in our lives.

So beyond providing a foundation for becoming a more effective adult educator, there are broader personal benefits to be derived from developing a working philosophy.

FOOTNOTES

1. John S. Brubacher, <u>Modern Philosophies of Education</u> (New York: McGraw-Hill Book Company, 1969), p. 1.

2. <u>Ibid</u>., p. 4.

3. <u>Ibid</u>., p. 5.

4. <u>Ibid</u>., p. 6.

5. <u>Ibid</u>.

6. David Riesman, <u>The Lonely Crowd</u> (New Haven: Yale University Press, 1950).

7. Gale Jensen, A.A.Liveright, and Wilbur Hallenbeck, <u>Adult Education--Outlines of an Emerging Field of University Study</u> (Washington: Adult Education Association of the U.S.A., 1964), p. 21.

8. Joseph R. Royce, <u>The Encapsulated Man</u> (Princeton, N.J.: D. Van Nostrand Company, Inc., 1964), p. 101.

Chapter 2

A WORKING PHILOSOPHY

This paper is written for adult educators--professors, students, administrators, and practitioners who want to further develop their personal working philosophy of adult education. The intent is not to discuss traditional and contemporary philosophies at length, though basic information about several philosophies will be presented. Looking at and thinking about established philosophies is one source of information we can use in developing our own working philosophies.

Working philosophy is defined here as an individual adult educator's system of beliefs. We will be concerned primarily with beliefs about various dimensions of adult education. But even with this narrower focus, other more basic beliefs will also be considered. The more basic beliefs often serve as foundations or complement beliefs we have about adult education.

General Philosophy

In the literature, philosophy is defined literally as a love for a high degree of knowledge. Most philosophers agree that they are confronted with three basic questions:

1. What is real? (Metaphysics.) How does one distinguish between appearances and what actually is? The sun appears to rise in the east, yet most people know that in reality it does not.

2. How do we know? (Epistemology.) What is knowledge and what are the sources of knowledge?

3. What is of value? (Axiology.) How does one decide what is right and what is wrong, what is good or bad?

Though these are basic philosophical questions, they give us direction in looking at various established philosophies, including our own working philosophy.

Content and Process

There are two dimensions to philosophy--a content dimension and a process dimension. The content dimension includes writings about various traditional and contemporary philosophies. The process dimension furnishes guides to thinking in a systematic and organized way. Thus, the content dimension gives us a source of information about various belief systems; the process dimension provides us with an approach for analyzing our own and other belief systems.

Beliefs

As a foundation for thinking about our own working philosophy

7

(belief system), let's first look at the nature and sources of beliefs. How do we come to have the beliefs we now hold? Where do we get new beliefs? How do beliefs relate to values and attitudes?

Bem says, "If a man perceives some relationship between two things or between one thing and a characteristic of it, he is said to hold a belief."[1]

For example, both planes and autos will transport us, so we have a common belief about both these transportation modes -- they will carry us to some destination. Or we may believe that all Republicans are conservative and all Democrats are liberal. We have a belief about each of these political parties.

Sources of Beliefs

We obtain beliefs basically from two sources:

1. From what we experience.

2. From an authority.

When we experience something, we may immediately develop a belief about that experience. We may also reflect on that experience and logically derive additional beliefs. We may also get beliefs from intuition, the subconscious mind providing us with insightful interpretations of our various experiences.

And we get beliefs from an authority. We may be told what to believe by a parent, a friend, someone in high position, or someone who has previously experienced the situation.

For example, when we were very young, our parents probably told us that eating green apples might make us sick. Or a friend told us how sick he got when he ate green apples. Some of us accepted that and avoided green apples. But many of us chose to eat them anyway and thus formed our beliefs directly from the experience. Those more daring may even have tried many different kinds of green apples, and learned that not all of them made one sick. We may also have reflected on the series of experiences and decided that green plums should also be avoided as well as green pears. In Chapter 7, "Beliefs About Content," the various routes to knowledge are explained in greater detail.

Levels of Beliefs

We hold beliefs at various levels. Bem describes primitive and higher order beliefs.[2] Our primitive beliefs are obtained by a combination of what authorities have told us and what we have experienced over time.

Within primitive beliefs Bem differentiates zero-order and first-order beliefs. Zero-order beliefs are those we so much take for granted that we don't even know we have them. One zero-order belief is our faith in the validity of our sensory experiences, expressed in many ways. "Let me see it and then I'll believe it," is something most of us have said at one time or another. Other examples of zero-order beliefs are assumptions that things exist even when we aren't there to see them, or believing that gravity won't let us fly off the face of the earth no matter where we might be visiting. Usually we are not aware that there could be an alternative for our zero-order beliefs. It has not occurred to us, for example, that there may be a place on this earth where gravity wouldn't continue to hold us in its grip, or that gravitational pull might one day cease.

We are usually aware of first-order beliefs because we can imagine an alternative to them. We accept that water flows downhill, but could imagine that it might conceivably flow uphill- - at least the alternative is something we are aware of.

Higher Order Beliefs

Higher order beliefs are usually derived in one of the following ways, according to Bem:[3]

1. From a statement made by an authority whose credibility legitimizes transference from what he states to what we believe. For example, we may reason as follows:

   > Thorndike said that adults can learn.
   > Thorndike was a noted researcher in adult education.
   > Therefore, adults can learn.

2. Reasoning inductively from our experience.

   > Several adults attended a series of woodworking classes.
   > These adults were able to construct a piece of furniture
   >   after the series.
   > Therefore, adults can learn.

3. Building on premises that are themselves conclusions of prior syllogisms.

   > Adults can learn.
   > Adults have many needs.
   > Needs relate to motivation for learning.
   > Adults learn best when the learning situation relates to
   >   their needs.

Some higher order beliefs can be discounted by destroying any of their underlying premises. If, for example, we learned through documented study that Thorndike had made serious mistakes in his research on adult learning, we might be inclined to discount our conclusion that adults can learn. But here is where another dimension becomes important. Beliefs have more than a vertical dimension --they are not only based on the premises which immediately precede them, but may also be related horizontally to other beliefs and premises.

9

Though we may discount Thorndike's research, we still have the evidence of the woodworking class to substantiate our conviction that adults can learn. These are, of course, extremely simple examples to make the point; we may have hundreds of pieces of evidence on which to base our belief that adults can learn. Simply destroying one or more of these premises has, in the long run, little effect in altering our suppositions about adult learning. The interrelatedness of the premises supporting many beliefs are extremely complex, which is one reason why their modification is difficult.

Many of our beliefs have an evaluative dimension too. We hold some of our beliefs as good or desirable; we have placed a value on them. Thus they are more than simply a description of what we believe to be true. The statement, "Adults should learn the classics," is an evaluative belief. "Adult educators should be involved in social action programs," is another evaluative belief.

A word about the relationship of beliefs to attitudes, and to values. "A belief differs from a value, in that while a value concerns what a person regards as good or desirable, a belief is a statement of what he regards as true and factual."[4]

Of course, as mentioned earlier, some beliefs have a value dimension and the line between what is a belief and what is a value is often fuzzy. Bem defines a value as ". . .a primitive preference for or a positive attitude toward certain end-states of existence (like equality, salvation, self-fulfillment, or freedom), or certain broad modes of conduct (like courage, honesty, friendship, or chastity)."[5]

Attitude is defined as a like or dislike of something or someone. More precisely, "An attitude involves a positive or negative evaluation and a readiness to respond to related objects or situations in a characteristic and predictable manner."[6]

In summary, then, values are what we accept as good or desirable, attitudes are what we like or dislike, and beliefs are what we assume to be true. We can believe something is true and like or not like it. We can believe that dieting will keep us more healthy, yet not like to do it. We can believe that exercise will keep us more healthy and like to exercise.

The relationship between values and beliefs and between values and attitudes is not as clear. Values are usually central to our beliefs and attitudes. Indeed, as we've said earlier, many beliefs have a strong value component and we label them value-beliefs.

Recognition, Analysis, Judgment, and Evaluation

Analysis of one's beliefs includes reviewing and classifying them into a meaningful order. Some, particularly zero-order beliefs, may need to be discovered before they can be analyzed. The only answer to a question about supposition in a certain area may be, "I've never thought about that before." Thus, recognition of a belief becomes the first step in analysis. (In some areas a person may hold no beliefs--this must be discovered too.)

Recognition, review, and classification of beliefs, though a good start, is obviously not enough. We must search for areas where beliefs are poorly understood or nonexistent, or are simply held dogmatically.

To judge beliefs, we can ask questions such as: What is the source of this belief? Is the evidence I have valid--is what I experienced correct? Have I had enough experiences related to this belief? If its source is authority, is the authority credible? Is what I accepted as a child as truth still true for me today?

After beliefs are identified, analyzed, and judged, they must be evaluated. Do my beliefs adequately serve my current needs? Or more specifically, do my beliefs adequately support my role as an adult educator?

Next is a suggested framework which may be used to identify, analyze, judge, and evaluate beliefs. As Socrates said, "The unexamined life is not worthy to be lived by a man."

A Framework for a Working Philosophy

Some people are disturbed by frameworks, claiming they put thoughts into boxes and stifle creative ways of looking at situations. In part this criticism is valid, especially if we become slaves to frameworks rather than vice versa. Frameworks should always be open to criticism and thus to change.

But we cannot get along without frameworks. They help us look at questions, to see the relationships among questions, to include important question areas; in short, to better organize our thinking. A framework thus becomes the skeleton on which we hang our ideas.

Following is one framework that may be used to look at a personal working philosophy of adult education. It is by no means the only one that can be used.

This framework includes four categories:

1. The Learner. To develop one's working philosophy of adult education, it is essential that beliefs about the learner be carefully analyzed, and if necessary, developed. Ultimately, no matter what kind of adult education we are involved with, our concern is for the adult learner. What then do we believe about the adult learner?

2. Overall purpose of Adult Education. What do we believe are the goals and objectives of adult education? What is adult education trying to accomplish and why? Is it necessary that adult

11

education have overall purposes?

3. Content or Subject Matter. What is to be learned? What are the sources of content? What do we believe about the role of content in adult education?

4. Learning Process. What do we believe about how adults learn? About providing opportunities for learning? About the role of instructional objectives in adult education?

Briefly, this is one framework that can be used to analyze and further develop a working philosophy of adult education. Later, the issues within each of these framework areas will be discussed in considerably more depth.

FOOTNOTES

1. Daryl J. Bem, Beliefs, Attitudes, and Human Affairs (Belmont, Calif.: Brooks/Cole Publishing Co., 1970) p. 4.

2. Ibid., pp. 4-13.

3. Ibid., pp. 10-11.

4. George A. Theodorson and Achilles G. Theodorson, A Modern Dictionary of Sociology (New York: Thomas Y. Crowell Company, 1969), p. 28.

5. Bem, Beliefs, Attitudes, and Human Affairs, p. 16.

6. Theodorson and Theodorson, A Modern Dictionary of Sociology, p. 19.

Chapter 3

GENERAL PHILOSOPHIES--A BRIEF LOOK

General and educational philosophies can thus serve as an idea
source for the development of our own working philosophies. Some
might argue that it is of no value to retreat into history for ideas, that
one should be able to develop his beliefs without depending on the historical past. Rollo May comments on this when he writes about man's
relation to the past: ". . .the more profoundly he (man) can confront
and experience the accumulated wealth in historical tradition, the more
uniquely he can at the same time know and be himself. "[1]

First, I'll briefly discuss four general philosophical systems using
as a framework the three basic philosophical questions--what is reality?
what is knowledge? and what is of value? The four systems are:

1. Realism.
2. Idealism.
3. Experimentalism.
4. Existentialism.

Following the discussion of these general philosophical systems, I'll
summarize the educational philosophies that have grown out of them.

Realism and idealism are considered traditional philosophies. They
". . . have a common point of view: the end is fixed, established by
authority outside and above the individual; within this framework the
individual is free to choose the means of achieving the end. "[2]

Experimentalism and existentialism are considered modern philosophies.
They too have a common viewpoint, but it is quite different from that of
the traditionalists. "Modernists held that means and ends are of the same
dimension--of equal worth--and that the individual is free to select both
the ends and the means to achieving them. "[3]

Thus, the basic difference between the traditional philosophies
(idealism and realism) and the modern philosophies (experimentalism
and existentialism) is the relationship of ends and means. For the
traditional philosophies, the ends are predetermined by an outside
authority and man only has a voice in the achieving of the ends. For the
modern philosophies, man has a voice in determining both the ends and
the means.

Idealism

One of the oldest philosophical systems, idealism goes back to ancient
India in the East and Plato in the West. Those who subscribe to idealism
believe the most important element in life is the human spirit, and that
all reality is reducible to the fundamental substance--spirit.

"All that is experienced by the mind is the result of an Ultimate

13

Intelligence. "[4]   The function of man's mind is thought of ". . . as a conceptual process of a miniature Ultimate Mind seeking reality, knowledge, and values. . .according to the ideal standards of Perfection of an Ultimate Mind. "[5] Everything is thought of as logically arranged, orderly, and purposeful. Truth is seen as absolute and never relative to the circumstances of society or individual judgment. Truth is always the same (eternal) and is based in ". . .the eternal, intelligent nature of God. "[6]

To the idealist, reality is a world of the mind; reality is not concerned with things physical. It does not consider material things as reality.

Idealists believe one can obtain knowledge in ways other than the scientific method. Faith, authoritarianism, and intuition are considered instruments of knowledge. One can know something through faith and accept it as knowledge even though this knowledge may be challenged with conflicting evidence. Other knowledge may be obtained through intuition, without involving reasoning. Man is considered moral when he lives according to the will of God--this is then a source of values for man.

Value is: Eternal; God is the source of all value.
These values are consistent, eternal ideas in the Mind
of God. The supreme, unchanging values are: truth,
goodness, beauty. These values exist in reality. [7]

Realism (also called Materialism or Naturalism)

In many ways the opposite of idealism, realism views the material world as real in and of itself. The sum total of reality for the realist is the physical world. Anything beyond the physical world is not held to be reality, thus that which is conceived in the mind is not considered reality.

Man is one with his material environment. He does not exist apart from nature as a spiritual being. Scientific realists accept the following propositions regarding man:

a. Monism. All things are resolvable into matter. This includes the mental processes of man. The social sciences can be reduced to the physical sciences in understanding humanity. This position affirms that all of science forms one family tree. At the very root of the tree is chemistry and physics. The brain of man is resolvable into the chemical and physical processes of brain matter in demonstrating mental processes. This theory is also described as reductionism.

b. Operationism. The validity of any proposition depends upon the validity of the procedures used in arriving at the proposition. The method of science must be applied in philosophy, in order to arrive at any valid knowledge about the nature of man. This method will exclude all speculative propositions based upon reason but not verifiable through controlled human experience. Therefore, assertions such as, "man has a soul," are meaningless because the concept of soul is not asserted through scientific procedures.

c.   Mechanism. The behavior of man and the nature of man can be understood without any appeal to a higher creating being. Man exists in a machine-like universe. He is a functioning organic machine in turn. In fact all living beings are elaborate chemical machines that can be understood in this mechanistic fashion. It is possible for the scientists to create life once the knowledge about the mechanical procedures that brought about a chemical nucleic acid capable of reproducing itself exists. Scientific realists claim this knowledge currently exists.

d.   Determinism. Everything that happens in the universe has a cause. These causes exist in the nature of material reality. Applied to man, scientific realists believe that freedom of action is nonexistent. The ethical tradition of self-determinism is denied. Every human act is determined by a chain of causes and effects which are brought about by the human environment and biological genetics. If one knew the experiences as well as the biological nature of the human being, it would be possible to predict what he must do. The individual cannot escape the determining element of his physical nature and social environment. [8]

Values are determined from nature.

As a result of observing nature, man comes to know natural laws which provide the basis for ethical and aesthetical value judgments. Values so derived from nature are permanent. Values will have a natural quality rather than a supernatural quality. [9]

Aesthetics is seen as the reflection of nature with nature providing the principles that govern appreciation of beauty.

Experimentalism

Experimentalism is an umbrella word covering those philosophies that insist on empirical verification of truth. Under experimentalism are included the philosophies of pragmatism, instrumentalism, and empiricism. The word progressivism is used in education to mean the same as experimentalism.

Experience and problem solving are key words for those who subscribe to the experimentalist philosophy. Speculation about reality is believed to be a useless activity. The experimentalists believe that our experiences reveal reality.

15

Man can know only through experience; because his
senses may mislead him it is necessary to subject his
sensations to the control of sense verification. In-
strumentalists differ from the early pragmatists in that
the test of worthwhileness is not individual growth.
The consequences of a proposition must be subjected
to the test of social verification. What is demonstrated
as social worthwhileness constitutes truth. Nothing can
be called true in "a priori" fashion. All things become true if the consequences are demonstrated as
socially worthwhile. However, the social consensus
of what is considered worthwhile will change with society.
Experience reveals that societies change. Therefore,
truth will change. [10]

There is thus no changeless knowledge, as is viewed by the idealist,
for example. It is only through experience that knowledge exists-- as an
interacting process between an individual and his environment.

Truth is thus seen as something that is functional, something that
can help man solve his problems. The experimentalists stress the importance of man learning the problem-solving process.

The scientific method, which is advocated for problem solving,
includes:

1. Recognizing a felt problem or need.

2. Gathering information.

3. Formulating hypotheses.

4. Testing the hypotheses.

5. Interpreting the results.

To the experimentalist, the total of experience is an end to the individual, never just a means. The experimentalist outlook is inter-
woven with the following three conceptions from Kilpatrick: [11]

1. Ideas mean only their consequence in experience.

2. Experience is essentially social in origin and predominantly
    social in purpose.

3. We find out what to expect in life by studying experimentally
    the uniformities within experience.

In so far as values are concerned, the experimentalists reject
absolutes which measure good and bad. Human experience is the basis
for testing values.

Therefore all values:

a. Are changeable. The consensus of society will vary with the
    changes that take place in society.

b. Are probable. Because of the limitations of human experience in the process of solving problems, values can never be absolutely true under each and every circumstance. What is considered valuable today may be worthless tomorrow.

c. Arise from social and individual need. The idea of good actions arises from important ethical or aesthetical needs.

d. Have public consequences. The final test of morality and aesthetics is the effect an act or object has upon society. Each of these activities exists only in the human context of social experience. An action is good if it is socially worthwhile.

e. Are not universal. The ethical action is never universal because societies differ, one from another. In aesthetics, public taste will vary with the culture. This is because the experiences of people in varying cultures are different.[12]

Existentialism

One of the newest philosophies, existentialism, came out of Europe after World War I. The Danish philosopher, Soren Kierkegaard (1813-1855) provided the foundation for existentialism when he wrote and taught about man's inner freedom to direct his own life. The philosophy did not become popular in this country until after World War II.

The existentialist philosophy in some respects is an attempt to cast off the traditional and the so-called contemporary philosophies. The existentialist, because of his stress on individualism and individual freedom, resents even being categorized into a philosophical system.

The basic premise of this philosophy is man's responsibility to himself for goal-setting and decision-making free from group norms. However, there is much divergence within the existentialist philosophy, with extreme individualism on the one hand, and considerable relationship of the individual to society on the other.

Generally though, existentialism is described as man acting freely to choose and decide what is significant for him.

His free choice results in determining what he becomes. Man therefore decides his own essence, which is continually becoming as a result of his actions. He is responsible for his own condition. Each action defines the nature of man that exists in his mind.[13]

. . . the individual is thrown on his resources and has great personal freedom. He can rely neither on the past, the lessons of history, nor on the wisdom of others; for although he may find these somewhat helpful in seeking answers, his own situation is particular and unique. As he is confronted by one situation after another the manner in which he chooses always entails a crucial consequence,

17

because he is creating by his choices the kind of being that he becomes. Along with his personal freedom, therefore, he alone bears the burden of responsibilities for his choices.[14]

Truth is determined by each person in terms of what is significant to him. There is no way to distinguish truth from error using objective criteria, for there are no objective criteria. To arrive at truth, each human must not be coerced by others; he must not be influenced by society.

The existentialist believes that man is alone responsible for his value system. But there is a dimension of responsibility. "Man is responsible for his own acts. These actions affect other human beings, and so a value choice includes a responsibility for the actions of others."[15]

Summary

Drawing in part from Johnson,[16] Figure 1 shows the relationship of the four philosophies to each other, indicating that there is some overlap among the philosophies of idealism, realism, and experimentalism, and that existentialism is apart from, yet dependent on, the other philosophies.

Relationship of Philosophies

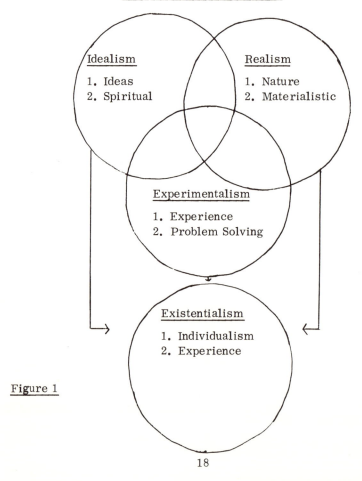

Figure 1

In Table 1, a summary of each of the four basic philosophies shows how the three questions: What is reality? What is truth? and What is of value? are answered.

Table 1

Summary of basic philosophies. *

	Reality	Truth	Values	
			Ethics	Aesthetics
Idealism	A world of mind	Truth as idea	Imitation of the Supreme being	Reflection of the Ideal
Realism	A world of things	Truth as observable fact	The law of nature	The reflection of nature
Experimentalism	A world of experience	Truth as what works	The public test	The public taste
Existentialism	A world of existing	Truth as existential choice	The anguish of freedom	The revolt from the public norm

*Table 1 was adopted from: Morris, Van Cleve. Philosophy and the American School (New York: Houghton Mifflin Company, 1961), pp. 466–67.

FOOTNOTES

1. Rollo May, Man's Search for Himself (New York: Signet Books, 1953), p. 179.

2. James C. Stone and Frederick W. Schneider, Foundations of Education (New York: Thomas Y. Crowell Co., Inc., 1971), p. 267.

3. Ibid.

4. Leo Charles Daley, Philosophy of Education (New York: College Notes, Inc., 1966), p. 49.

5. James Johnson, et. al., Introduction to the Foundations of American Education (Boston: Allyn and Bacon, 1969), p. 301.

6. Daley, Philosophy of Education, p. 50.

7. Ibid.

8. Ibid., p. 56.

9. Johnson, et. al. Introduction to the Foundations of American Education, p. 305.

10. Daley, _Philosophy of Education_, p. 68.

11. William H. Kilpatrick. "Philosophy of Education from the Experimentalist Outlook," in _Philosophies of Education, Forty-First Yearbook, National Society for the Study of Education_ (Bloomington, Illinois: Public School Publishing Co., 1942), p. 41.

12. Daley, _Philosophy of Education_, p. 69.

13. _Ibid._, p. 65.

14. Stone and Schneider, _Foundations of Education_, p. 286.

15. Daley, _Philosophy of Education_, pp. 65-66.

16. Johnson, et. al. _Introduction to the Foundations of American Education_, pp. 311-312.

Chapter 4

EDUCATIONAL PHILOSOPHIES--AN OVERVIEW

Over the years, educationalists and certain philosophers have developed several educational philosophies. These philosophies, though they are closely related to the general philosophies, deal more directly with educational problems. The following educational philosophies are briefly described:

1. Essentialism.
2. Perennialism.
3. Progressivism.
4. Reconstructionism.
5. Existentialism.

Essentialism

William C. Bagley is credited with the formulation of this educational philosophy in 1938. Since then it has become and continues to be a philosophy practiced in many schools in this country, and around the world.

According to the essentialists, the essential elements of education are available from historical and contemporary knowledge. This educational philosophy has roots in both idealism and realism. From the idealist's point of view, the content of education comes from such areas as history, foreign languages, and the classics. From the realist's viewpoint, the content of education is derived from the physical world, including mathematics and the natural sciences.

The essentialists subscribe to a traditional approach to education, a returning to the three R's. The methodology advocated by the essentialists includes much required reading, lectures, memorization, repetition, audio-visual materials, and examinations.

Essentialists see their role as one of preserving and passing on the culture to succeeding generations -- the prime emphasis is on subject matter.

Perennialism

Perennialists subscribe to the view that the basic beliefs and knowledge of the ancient culture have as much application today as they did thousands of years ago.

> The focus of learning in Perennialism lies in activities designed to discipline the mind. Subject matter of a disciplinary and spiritual nature such as the content of mathematics, languages, logic, great books, and doctrines must be studied whether used as such or not. [1]

Perennialism is also thought of as the parent philosophy of essentialism.

The perennialists, as do the essentialists, advocate such teaching approaches as memorization, reading, writing, drill, and recitation. There is heavy stress on "disciplining the mind," and the belief that learning can only occur if the mind is properly exercised.

Many perennialists also believe that education should be directed toward the intellectually gifted, and the less gifted be provided vocational training. Some perennialists, following Plato's suggestions, advocate that the leaders of the country be drawn from the intellectually elite.

The most popular present day application of the perennialist philosophy is the Great Books program promoted by Robert M. Hutchins and Mortimer Adler. The Great Books program suggests that studying the leading scholars of history is the way to obtain a general education, one that will have much application today.

Progressivism

Established in this country in the mid-1920's, progressivism is opposed to authoritarianism and favors man's experience as a basis for knowledge. This philosophy represents a response to both essentialism and perennialism, which were criticized because of their extreme authoritarian positions.

The progressivists give no emphasis to an absolute knowledge. To them all things are in a state of transition. This philosophy grew out of the pragmatism of Charles S. Peirce and William James, and was further developed for education by John Dewey.

Helping the student learn problem solving--how to think--is emphasized. Experimentalism provides the roots for the educational philosophy of progressivism, and thus the scientific method is stressed as a way of solving problems and discovering knowledge. Where the essentialist and the perennialist focus on subject matter, the progressivist focuses on the learning process. Where the essentialist and perennialist are preoccupied with perpetuating the culture, the progressivist is concerned with improving man's life in society.

> The learner is viewed as an experiencing, thinking, exploring individual. Progressivism exposes the learner to the subject matter of social experiences, social studies, projects, problems and experiments which, when studied by the scientific method, will result in functional knowledge from all subject matter areas. Books are regarded as tools in the learning process rather than as sources of indisputable knowledge.[2]

Reconstructionism

For some educational philosophers, reconstructionism is seen as a part of progressivism. There are similarities between the two philosophies. Both subscribe to the belief that values are man-made and relative to culture, time, and place. Both agree that the human experience generates fundamental values. But reconstructionism, expecially as expressed by Theodore Brameld, is more concerned with ends than means, and in this respect differs from progressivism. Some readers might immediately argue that reconstructionism is thus no different from essentialism and perennialism, which also focus on ends.

Reconstructionism differs from these traditional philosophies in how the ends are determined. The essentialists and perennialists rely on ends (truth) determined through nonempirical approaches. These ends (truths) are thus absolute with an eternal status.

The reconstructionists rely on the scientific method to discover truth and recognize that the ends (truths) will change as problems change and as new solutions to problems are discovered.

Existentialism

The basic view of this educational philosophy is that education should be directed toward individual self-fulfillment. George Kneller describes existentialism as follows:

> To begin, it rules out three conventional notions: that
> education is primarily an agency of society, set up to
> perpetuate a cultural heritage; that it is a pipe line
> of perennial truths; and that it is a means for adjusting
> the young to life in a democratic community. In place
> of these, let education exist for the individual. Let it
> teach him to live as his own nature bids him, spontaneously
> and authentically.[3]

To the existentialist, education is viewed as an instrument for encouraging maximum individual choice and autonomy. What a person is capable of knowing and experiencing is more important that what he knows.

Brubacher says this about an existentialist philosophy of education:

> To the extent . . . [it]. . .has been projected, it is
> not unlike the pragmatic. It depends heavily upon
> the student's own experience in meeting particular
> situations. Left alone to confront them, he is
> encouraged to encounter them head-on, for it is in
> taking action in human crises that he develops self-
> reliance in overcoming despair. Similarly, it is
> through committing himself to intervene in the
> situation that values emerge. By no means are values

preexistent to action and thus waiting to be discovered.[4]

Harper stresses the importance of existentialism focusing on the whole person in the situation in which the person finds himself.

> This implies two things; first, that there is some sense
> in speaking of the individual as a whole, of man as a whole
> and, second, that individuals cannot be considered indepen-
> dently of their situations. The whole man or woman or
> child, within the environment of time and place that he is
> born into--this is the object of education, or the subject.
> The unfolding, the development of this subject, is the end
> which the existentialist works towards.[5]

Harper says the existentialist is primarily concerned with ". . . encouraging individuals of all kinds and conditions to understand their situation and themselves."[6]

Discussion

There is obviously no clear agreement as to which educational philosophy should be followed. There are those who criticize formal education in this country for being too progressivist oriented, and argue that we must return to a more traditional educational approach. Harry Boudy and John Palmer said the following about progressive education:

> A technically sophisticated society simply does not
> dare leave the acquisition of systematized knowledge
> to concomitant learning, the by-product of projects that
> are themselves wholesome slices of juvenile life. In-
> telligence without systematized knowledge will do only
> for the most ordinary, everyday problems. International
> amity, survival in our atomic age, automation, racial
> integration, are not common everyday problems to
> which common-sense knowledge and a sense of decency
> are adequate.[7]

The problem-solving technique of progressive education is criticized for discovering the wheel over and over again. Some critics ask, "If something is found out, some solution to a problem is known, why go through the motions of discovering for the millionth time simply so someone can have the thrill of discovery?"

Still others, anxious to preserve as a prime goal of education passing on the culture from one generation to the next, insist that educating be done as inexpensively and as efficiently as possible. To these critics problem solving takes too much time, and besides, these critics say, many important truths may never be learned for there are no problems to fit them.

On the other hand the traditional philosophers, perennialists, and essentialists are chastised because they tend to develop the majority of people into dependent followers more likely to carry out orders than to criticize or approve them.

Other critics of the traditional philosphies argue that they advocate simply an accumulation of information. . . whether it is useful or not to the learner makes no difference.

From a humanistic viewpoint, the traditional philosophies are taken to task because someone other than the learner is making decisions about what he will learn and how he will learn it. Who has the right to make decisions about which "essential" knowledge should be passed on, to whom? Who has the right to decide the order of things, which knowledge should be taught, and how it should be taught? These kinds of questions are asked of the perennialists and the essentialists.

The progressivists, besides being criticized from the outside, recognize problems within their ranks. Brameld summarizes two of the issues, the relationship between ends and means and the relationship between the individual and society.

> If we are not to turn back from liberalism-progressivism to
> either the conservative-essentialist or the regressivist-
> perennialist alternative, both of which have strong appeal
> for some individuals and some powerful groups, both of
> which deserve to be heard with the care and respect. . ., our
> task is not to reject but to reexamine, correct, and supple-
> ment liberalism-progressivism as fully and forthrightly
> as possible. Basic to our task is the diagnosis of two
> spheres of tension that are, we believe, chronic to this
> theory and program: one, the tension between means and ends;
> the other, the tension between individuality and sociality.
> The great opportunity that now rises before citizens and
> teachers in search of philosophy of life and education appro-
> priate to our revolutionary age is to consider how each of
> these tensions can be at once utilized and constructively
> released: the tension between means and ends, through
> courageous commitments, convictions, and future-centered
> purposes, which, in the course of their attainment, strengthen
> and refine scientific methodology; the tension between indi-
> viduality and sociality, through relentless analysis of cul-
> tural obstacles, through aggressive social strategies, and
> through enhancement of the values of the individual in the
> normative matrix of a designed world order and a planned
> democratic culture. [8]

Paulo Freire views education as a means for people to free themselves from oppression and participate together in the transformation of society.

He is critical of educators who follow the traditional philosophies.

Narration (with the teacher as narrator) leads the students

to memorize mechanically the narrated content. Worse yet, it turns them into 'containers,' into 'receptacles' to be 'filled' by the teacher. The more completely he fills the receptacles, the better a teacher he is. The more meekly the receptacles permit themselves to be filled, the better students they are.

Education thus becomes an act of depositing, in which the students are depositories and the teacher is the depositor. Instead of communicating, the teacher issues communiques and makes deposits which the students patiently receive, memorize, and repeat. This is the 'banking' concept of education, in which the scope of action allowed to the students extends only as far as receiving, filling, and storing the deposits. They do, it is true, have the opportunity to become collectors or catalogers of the things they store. But in the last analysis, it is men themselves who are filed away through the lack of creativity, transformation, and knowledge of this (at best) misguided system. For apart from inquiry, apart from the praxis, men cannot be truly human. Knowledge emerges only through invention and re-invention, through the restless, impatient, continuing, hopeful inquiry men pursue in the world, with the world, and with each other. [9]

What is your stand, as an adult educator, on these issues? Is it important that a body of essential truths be passed on, perhaps those truths that were missed during the formal school years? Do you subscribe to the progressivist approach, helping adults as they face the problems of living to solve these problems? Do you agree with the reconstructionist's point of view? Are there some definite ends that you as an adult educator should work toward, to better the status of people and improve society?

How about the view of the existentialists? Do you believe that education is a means for encouraging maximum individual choice and autonomy, that education can help individuals understand their situations and themselves?

These issues and others will be discussed in more depth as we move on toward discussing a working philosophy of adult education.

Contribution from General and Educational Philosophies

What use can you make of the ideas presented in the general and educational philosophies as you think about your own working philosophy? There are several alternatives:

1. You can select one of the educational philosophies as your own, completely and entirely.

2. You can select pieces from several philosophies and fashion an eclectic philosophy of your own. There are dangers in doing this, however. Because the basic premises of the philosophies vary, the eclectic approach may lead to a selection of beliefs that contradict each other. If you assert, for example, that man should strive to solve the problems of living by applying knowledge that contributes to solutions, it is difficult to also believe, without contradiction, that there is essential knowledge that every man should be taught with no regard to the usefulness of that knowledge.

3. You can agree not to select any one philosophy, nor put together an eclectic one. You may simply leave the issue open and follow whichever beliefs seem appropriate at the moment.

4. You can, through an analytical process which focuses on major issue areas in adult education, strive to analyze your present working philosophy, and build on it where necessary. The general and educational philosophies can furnish ideas for your working philosophy, but you don't use the ideas until they have been subjected to careful analysis and study.

Lindeman has an interesting insight as he quotes and comments on Anatole France:

'Each of us, ' wrote Anatole France, 'must be allowed to possess two or three philosophies at the same time, ' for the purpose, I presume, of saving our thought from the deadly formality of consistency. No one can write about education, particularly adult education, without deserting at various points all 'schools' of pedagogy, psychology, and philosophy. Incongruities are obvious: one cannot for example, be a determinist and at the same time advocate education; nor can idealism be made to fit the actualities of life without recognition of the material limitations which surround living organisms. One cannot, that is, make use of these opposed points of view if they are conceived to be mutually-exclusive. [10]

Then Lindeman says, "Light comes from learning--just as creation comes everywhere--through integrations, syntheses, not through exclusions. "[11]

FOOTNOTES

1. James Johnson et. al., <u>Introduction to the Foundations of American Education</u> (Boston: Allyn and Bacon, 1969), p. 322.

2. <u>Ibid</u>., p. 327.

3. George Kneller, "Education, Knowledge, and the Problem of Existence, " <u>Harvard Educational Review,</u> XXXI (Fall, 1961), p. 42.

27

4. John S. Brubacher, <u>Modern Philosophies of Education</u> (New York: McGraw-Hill Book Company, Inc., 1962), p. 322.

5. Ralph Harper, "Significance of Existence and Recognition for Education," in <u>Modern Philosophies of Education,</u> ed. by Nelson B. Henry (Chicago: National Society for the Study of Education, 1955), p. 223.

6. <u>Ibid.</u>, p. 227.

7. Harry S. Broudy and John R. Palmer, <u>Exemplars of Teaching Method</u> (Chicago: Rand McNally, 1965).

8. Johnson, et. al., <u>Introduction to the Foundations,</u> p. 329.

9. Paulo Freire, <u>Pedagogy of the Oppressed</u> (New York: Herder and Herder, 1970), p. 58.

10. Edward C. Lindeman, <u>The Meaning of Adult Education</u> (Montreal: Harvest House, 1961), p. XXVII.

11. <u>Ibid.</u>

Chapter 5

BELIEFS ABOUT THE ADULT LEARNER

Fundamentally, what do we believe about the adult learner? In the most basic sense, what is the nature of human nature? There are many issues related to these questions, considerably more than are mentioned here. I therefore suggest several matters that interest me and seem important. At the end of this chapter, I've included several references recommended to the reader who wants to get deeper into the issues mentioned and perhaps delve into problems I haven't touched upon at all.

One of the most basic issues is the mind-body problem. "Of what is man made? It has long been the common-sense view of our culture that the nature of man is dualistic, that man is composed of mind and body, spirit and flesh."[1] There are obviously problems for the educator if this belief is accepted as is. How can an educator provide educational opportunity for the mind when often the body, at the same time, is demanding food or physical activity?

Some educators, in an attempt to reconcile this difficulty, have tried to simplify human nature by considering it either all mind or all body. The realists, for example, lean toward the view that all mental functions can be reduced to bodily functions. The idealists, on the other hand, suggest that everything is a function of the mind. "To them nothing gives a greater sense of reality than the activity of mind engaged in trying to comprehend its world."[2] A third group of educators has tried to deal with human nature as an integral whole with an interrelationship between mind and body.

Contemporary writers continue to disagree about the mind-body problem. B. F. Skinner suggests that the idea of an autonomous man free to make decisions, free to have freedom and dignity, is an outmoded idea. Further, he suggests that we must do away with the concepts of mind states and feelings. He writes:

> As the interaction between organism and environment
> has come to be understood, however, effects once
> assigned to states of mind, feelings, and traits are
> beginning to be traced to accessible conditions, and
> a technology of behavior may therefore become available.
> It will not solve our problems, however, until it
> replaces traditional prescientific views, and these
> are strongly entrenched. Freedom and dignity illustrate
> the difficulty. They are the possessions of the autonomous
> man of traditional theory, and they are essential to
> practices in which a person is held responsible for his
> condition and given credit for his achievements. A
> scientific analysis shifts both the responsibility and
> the achievement to the environment.[3]

Carl Rogers suggests we must move toward giving more freedom to the learner. He says:

> I like it when I can permit freedom to others, and in this
> I think I have learned, and developed considerable ability.
> I am frequently, though not always, able to take a group,
> a course, or a class of students, and to set them
> psychologically free. I can create a climate in which they
> can be and direct themselves.[4]

Skinner says we must do away with individual freedom; Rogers says we must have more of it. Skinner suggests the free thinking, non-directed man is a thing of the past; Rogers insists it is only through individual thought that man will be able to learn.

Skinner discounts the importance of mind beyond the biological characteristics of the brain and the nervous system--thus a tendency toward seeing mind and body as one biological unit. Rogers, on the other hand, accepts the importance of the non-biological dimensions of the mind and tends toward resolving the dualistic problem of mind-body by dealing with the whole man. His writings support his belief in a close interrelationship between mind and body.

Another long-time issue in any discussion about the nature of man is the moral question. Is human nature essentially good, or is it essentially bad? Is the question of goodness and badness one that can be placed on a continuum with good on one end and bad on the other? Or is human nature neither good nor bad?

Those who believe that human nature is essentially bad say that man's nature is to avoid learning, that he is lazy and undisciplined. He is dependent on some outside authority for his feelings and ideas and without this outside authority he would be nothing.

The opposing position is that man is basically good.

> According to Rousseau, human nature as it came from
> the hands of its Maker was essentially good. To be
> sure, it was immature and had weaknesses that needed
> correcting through education, but even so the material
> the parent and teacher had to work with was basically
> good.[5]

The third view is that man is neither good nor bad by nature. "What the individual becomes is not the result of any innate predisposition but is the result of what he learns to become."[6] What man becomes is the result of the experiences he has had, all of which produce learning. ". . . human nature will be seen to have both strengths and weaknesses, but just which they are will depend on the environmental context. . ."[7]

Two other issues that interest me, particularly from the viewpoint of the adult learner, are the question of man's relationship to society, and man's relationship to the natural world.

Relationship to Society

Here I am intrigued by issues in two areas: (1) the extent to which man is totally a part of society versus being in some degree apart from society, and (2) the influence relationships between man and society. The two alternatives in (1) may be diagrammed as shown in Figure 2.

Man and Society

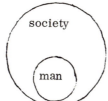

A. Man totally a part of society.

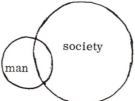

B. Man, to a degree, apart from society.

Figure 2

This leads to questions about the influence relationship between man and society. If man is totally a part of society as in Figure 2A, what are the influence relationships? Does society totally influence the course of life which man follows? Or does man have some influence on the society in which he is totally immersed? Is there an opportunity for an interacting relationship, with man influencing the society and the society influencing the man?

The same questions can be raised about Figure 2B.

1. Does society totally influence man as illustrated in Figure 3A?

2. Does man totally influence society as in Figure 3B?

3. Is there an interaction between man and society as in Figure 3C?

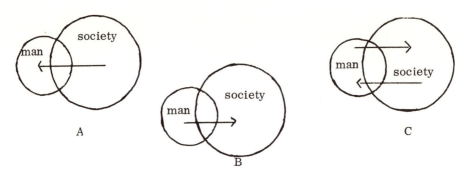

Man and Society Influence Relationships

Figure 3

Position A is held by those who subscribe to the concept of "other
directed man,"[8] which says that all of what man does is influenced by
others. Position B is the "rugged individual" concept. Man as he makes
decisions and carries them out influences society, and society then
becomes the sum of these individual influences. Position C suggests
the influence relationship is an interacting one between man and society.

Relationship to the Natural World

Many writers combine society and the natural world and talk about
man's relationship to his environment. I believe there are sufficient
differences in the relationship of man to society, and man to the natural
world (defined to include the total ecosystem), that we must deal with
our beliefs in each of these areas separately.

The questions about the relationship to the natural world are similar
to the questions about man's relationship to society:

1. The extent man is totally a part of nature, totally divorced
    from nature, or partially outside of nature, and partially
    included (Figure 4).

2. The influence relationship of man to nature.

These three questions related to 1 may be diagrammed as in
Figure 4:

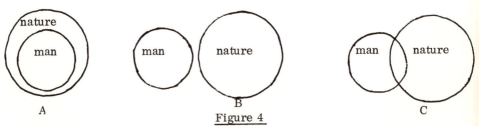

Figure 4

Diagram A represents the belief that man is continuous with the
natural world, that he is a part of nature and no different from any other

32

living matter. Man is one kind of animal, living among many other kinds of animals and other living matter, and is seen as basically no different from any other animal. The same techniques used to study animals would be equally applicable when used to study man.

Diagram B represents the belief that man and nature are completely divorced, that they exist totally apart from each other. Man through his inventive genius, has been able to transcend nature and is able to control his physical environment to the extent that he need not be concerned with the natural world.

The third alternative, Diagram C, represents the belief that man is in part integral with the natural world, that he does have biological characteristics which make him similar to other living matter--he has need for food, water, air, etc. But man also has a mind and intellect that set him apart from the natural world. Man has the ability to reflect on his experience, a characteristic no other living being has. He can recall the past, and use the knowledge of the past in acting on the present and in planning for the future. Man thus has a consciousness about his life that makes him different from other animals.

There are several questions of man's relationship to his natural world related to each of the orientations explained before. First, if we believe that man is totally apart from nature (as in Figure 4B):

1. Does nature have any control over man?

2. Does man totally control nature?

3. Is there a potential for an interacting influence between man and nature?

The following figure illustrates these relationships:

Man and Nature Influence Relationships

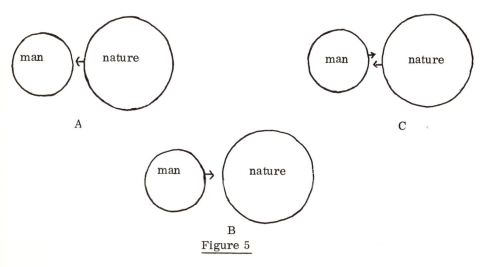

Figure 5

If we believe that man is continuous with nature (Figure 4A), that he is just another living creature among many, then can man's influence on the natural world be any greater than that of any other living creature? Of course we quickly recognize that every living creature does not influence the natural world in the same way nor to the same degree. But can the way that man influences the natural world be any different than the way other living creatures influence the natural world?

If we believe that man is in part integral with the natural world and in part separate from the natural world (Figure 4C), what are the relationships?

The following figure illustrates them:

Man and Nature Influence Relationships

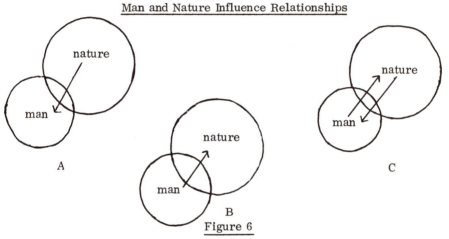

Figure 6

Figure 6A--does nature totally influence man? Figure 6B--does man totally influence nature? Figure 6C--is there an interacting influence of man and nature?

Discussion

These are but a few of the questions that may be raised about the basic nature of man. How we answer them determines our beliefs about the nature of the adult learner. As we deal with more issues about the nature of the learner, our belief system becomes more complete.

The beliefs we have about the adult learner relate directly to the other elements in our working philosophy framework. If we believe, for example, that man is basically bad, is dualistic, that his body and mind are considered separately, that he is totally a part of society and totally controlled by nature, we are led to specific conclusions about the adult in a learning situation. We will reach different conclusions about how to deal with the adult if our beliefs about his basic nature are different from the example just given.

A similar logic can be followed as we think through our beliefs about the objectives of adult education, and its content or subject matter.

FOOTNOTES

1. James S. Brubacher, Modern Philosophies of Education (New York: McGraw-Hill, 1962), p. 46.

2. Ibid., p. 47.

3. B. F. Skinner, Beyond Freedom and Dignity (New York: Alfred A. Knopf, 1971), p. 25.

4. Carl R. Rogers, Freedom to Learn (Columbus, Ohio: Charles E. Merrill, 1969), p. 232.

5. Brubacher, Modern Philosophies of Education, p. 71.

6. Tom C. Venable, Philosophical Foundations of the Curriculum (Chicago: Rand McNally, 1967), p. 34.

7. Brubacher, Modern Philosophies of Education, p. 72.

8. See David Riesman, The Lonely Crowd (New Haven: Yale University Press, 1950), for a discussion of the concept.

Related Reading

1. James Gribble, Introduction to Philosophy of Education (Boston: Allyn and Bacon, 1969).

2. Marvin Farber, Basic Issues of Philosophy (New York: Harper Torchbooks, 1968).

3. Adrian Dupuis, ed., Nature, Aims, and Policy (Urbana, Illinois: University of Illinois Press, 1970).

4. John R. Platt, ed., New Views of the Nature of Man (Chicago: University of Chicago Press, 1965).

5. Donald Vandenburg, Being and Education (Englewood Cliffs, New Jersey: Prentice-Hall, 1971).

6. Steven M. Cahn, The Philosophical Foundations of Education (New York: Harper and Row, 1970).

7. Thomas O. Buford, Toward a Philosophy of Education (New York: Holt, Rinehart, & Winston, 1969).

8. James L. Jarrett, Philosophy for the Study of Education (New York: Houghton Mifflin Company, 1969).

9. A. H. Maslow, The Farther Reaches of Human Nature (New York: The Viking Press, 1971).

10. Joseph R. Royce, The Encapsulated Man (Princeton, N.J.: D. Van Nostrand Company, 1964).

11. Rollo May, Man's Search for Himself (N.Y.: New American Library, 1953).

Chapter 6

BELIEFS ABOUT THE OVERALL PURPOSE OF ADULT EDUCATION

What do we believe are the purposes of adult education? What do we believe they should be? Houle,[1] in his analysis of the field of adult education, describes five orientations held by different groups of adult educators that relate to the question of purpose (he calls them credos):

(1) Centering on a goal. There are those in adult education who believe ". . . that adult education should be a movement unified by a common effort to achieve a single all encompassing goal."[2] Examples of these goals include liberal education, humanistic education, and cultivation of the human mind.

(2) Meeting needs and interests. A large group of adult educators believe that people know what they need to know, ". . . and the task of the adult educator is to discover what that is and provide it for them."[3]

(3) Adapting schooling. Elementary, secondary and higher education should be provided for adults as it is for children, in a similar form.

(4) Strengthening leadership. The focus of adult education should be on developing strong leaders in the field. "The creator of an institution or movement, such as Bishop Grundtvig, Jane Addams, or Seaman Knapp--uses the force of personality to achieve the ends sought."[4]

(5) Improving adult education institutions. These adult educators focus on improving operations within adult education institutions and improving relationships among institutions.

(6) Increasing informality. "Many educators of adults conceive of themselves as enemies of systematization, particularly as it is manifested in childhood-youth education."[5]

Bergevin is quite specific in what he considers to be the purposes of adult education:

1. To help the learner achieve a degree of happiness and meaning in life;

2. To help the learner understand himself; his talents and limitations, and his relationships with other persons;

3. To help adults recognize and understand the need for life-long learning;

4. To provide conditions and opportunities to help the adult advance in the maturation process spiritually, culturally, physically, politically, and vocationally;

5. To provide, where needed, education for survival, in literacy, vocational skills, and health measures."[6]

There are many questions that can be raised about the purposes of adult education. As we think about the general and educational philosophies, reflect on adult education practice today, and review the speculations of contemporary authors, we get many, often opposing, points of view.

Is the purpose of adult education:

1. To help people make psychological adjustments to their social conditions and natural world by equipping them with the necessary knowledge, understanding, skills, and attitudes?

This viewpoint grows out of the essentialist and perennialist philosophies of education which assume there are essential elements of education, and that the basic beliefs and knowledge of former cultures are applicable today. This viewpoint is sometimes expressed as passing on the culture from one generation to the next. The experiences of our ancestors in meeting the problems of living, for example, are "taught" so man today doesn't have to discover solutions to problems which have already been solved. Of course there is always the difficulty of knowing, from the "teacher" point of view, if the problems of living today are sufficiently similar to those of the past so the solutions from the past will fit. Those who adhere to this objective believe that there are knowledge, understandings, skills, and attitudes that apply to a wide variety of situations, not only the situations where there was application in the past.

2. To equip adults with the skills necessary for identifying and solving problems they may face with an emphasis on the skills in solving problems and not on the content or subject matter?

The progressivist philosophy of education is the source of this viewpoint which focuses on man's experience as a basis for knowledge. What is important is that the learner learn how to think, learn how to identify his problems; and then through a problem-solving process, using knowledge as a tool, solve these problems.

There is an assumed two-pronged end- - solving the problem, and learning the means for problem solving. Learning the means for solving problems is as important an end as is the solution to the problem. Acquisition of knowledge is secondary; its importance lies in its use in contributing to the solution of problems. Both the means and the actual problem solution are seen as equally important ends.

3. To help people change their social conditions?

Is it the role of adult education to help people initiate changes in society which may not have otherwise occurred, or perhaps wouldn't have occurred so soon, or in the direction that people desired?

This position comes from the reconstructionist philosophy of education and places more emphasis on the end (a changed society) than on the means of achieving the end. The means used are the same ones advocated by the progressivists. But where the progressivist, as explained above, puts equal emphasis on means and ends--or at least tries to--the reconstructionist puts more emphasis on ends.

This viewpoint of helping people change social conditions is one of the most controversial in adult education today. And it often polarizes adult educators into two camps--those who feel the purpose of adult education should be for individual growth and development, and those who feel adult education can be a force in transforming society. Paulo Freire[7] suggests to this writer that through a process of changing society, man can grow and develop personally. Reading Freire, this writer concludes that the polarity between individual growth and societal change is a false issue.

4. To help people become free, autonomous individuals?

Growing primarily out of the existentialist movement, this view suggests that the overriding purpose of adult education should be directed toward individual self-fulfillment and freedom. There is a continuum of positions within this point of view. On the one end of the continuum are those who believe that the purpose of adult education should be to provide maximum freedom and choice for the individual--what a person learns is what he wants to learn. The other end of the continuum combines individual freedom with responsibility for the society.

Harper says, "The real meaning of human freedom is that it arises from and is directed toward an order of reality which is primarily beyond any human circle. If it were not, man would have to feed on himself as animals feed on their own powers and needs. Whenever men have tried to use themselves as ends, or shrink their world-view to a view of self, their isolation becomes so cramped that their whole reflective apparatus slows down and revolts or becomes paralyzed. The world and truth are the bright goals of free man.

To say that a man should devote himself to the world and truth is not to say that he should lose self or freedom. In a sense, he should lose himself only to find himself; the curriculum is there for him."[8]

Other contemporary authors in this area include A.H. Maslow,[9] Carl Rogers,[10] Rollo May,[11] Eric Fromm,[12] and Martin Buber.[13]

Discussion

There are many questions that can be asked about overall purposes for adult education. A basic one is, should adult educators seek overall purposes for the field? Is the field so broad that overall purposes are not only impossible to determine, but may stifle the activities of individual adult education efforts? Should the overall purpose of adult education thus be to encourage multiple purposes?

If, however, you believe there should be overall purposes, what is your stand on the four purposes listed above? Do you believe they should all be emphasized, or only one or two of them? Should all of these purposes be emphasized, but some emphasized more than others?

As we analyze the four objectives listed above, we can ask if they are compatible with each other. Can adult education at the same time advocate passing on the culture and work toward the improvement of society? Can freedom and self-fulfillment come from working with others toward the improvement of society? Can a person achieve freedom and self-fulfillment without working with others toward the improvement of society? Is it important that people be "taught" certain attitudes, knowledge, and skills that a society believes they need, though some people may not feel a need for learning these attitudes, knowledge, and skills at the time they are offered? What criteria does an educator use to determine what someone else needs?

As we think about purposes, many more questions will no doubt surface. Let the above be a starting place.

FOOTNOTES

1. Cyril O. Houle, The Design of Education (San Francisco: Jossey-Bass Inc., 1972).

2. Ibid., p. 7.

3. Ibid., p. 7.

4. Ibid., p. 8.

5. Ibid., pp. 255-56.

6. Paul Bergevin, A Philosophy for Adult Education (New York: The Seabury Press, 1967), pp. 30-31.

7. Paulo Freire, Pedagogy of the Oppressed (New York: Herder and Herder, 1970).

8. Ralph Harper, "Significance of Existence and Recognition for Education," in Modern Philosophies and Education, ed. by Nelson B. Henry (Chicago: National Society for the Study of Education, 1955), p. 233.

9. A.H. Maslow, The Farther Reaches of Human Nature (New York: The Viking Press, 1971).

10. Carl Rogers, Freedom to Learn (Columbus, Ohio: Charles E. Merrill, 1969).

11. Rollo May, Man's Search for Himself (New York: New American Library, 1953).

12. Eric Fromm, The Art of Loving (New York: Harper and Row, 1956).

13. Martin Buber, I and Thou (New York: Charles Scribner's Sons, 1958).

Chapter 7

BELIEFS ABOUT CONTENT

Two of the oldest philosophical questions in education are what should be taught and how do we determine what should be taught? Or in reference to adult education, what is subject matter for adult learners? How should this subject matter be determined?

First, the question of subject matter for adult learners and some of the issues associated with it:

1. Is subject matter or knowledge of value by itself?

2. Is there something inherently good in knowledge?

3. Is there certain knowledge that everyone should have, no matter what?

4. Is knowledge only of value when it helps one to solve his problems?

5. Is knowledge only of value when it helps one to become free, to help one move toward self-actualization?

The essentialists and perennialists would answer yes to questions one through three. They would argue that there is a great body of knowledge that has stood the test of time and should be passed on from one generation to the next. And for man to be a functioning individual in society, he must accumulate much of this knowledge.

The progressivists and reconstructionists believe there is no ultimate or absolute knowledge that should be passed on from one generation to another. To them knowledge is something that works. ". . .the test of truth is to be found in the here and now of human experience. If a thing aids human experience, it is true; if it thwarts and stifles experience it is false."[1]

For the existentialist, knowledge is gained through experience and is relative to the individual. It is for each person to decide what is significant and true for him.

There are criticisms of each of these positions. Those who believe there is eternal knowledge are criticized because their focus is on subject matter and not on people. The question is: Why should someone learn something that may never be of use to him? Of course, the larger questions are what does "use to him" mean and who knows what might be useful to someone at any given point in his life? And can someone always know, by himself, what is and what is not useful to him? Do people have needs for knowledge which they themselves cannot identify? Is it reasonable to expect that people will store knowledge, which at some later time may be of use to them? Or should knowledge be available, and when a person has a need for it, he goes looking for the appropriate knowledge to help him? Should knowledge be stored in books, or in people?

Another criticism of the essentialist and perennialist positions is that someone doesn't really have knowledge unless he has tested it against reality. Can someone "know" swimming without ever getting into a swimming pool? How can someone be sure the knowledge he has about swimming is true unless he has experienced swimming himself?

Still another criticism is the contradictions that often exist among authorities. Which knowledge is true if several knowledge sources disagree with each other?

Similarly, there are many who are skeptical of the progressivist, reconstructionist, and existentialist views about knowledge. Venable summarizes criticisms of the progressivist approach: "The chief critcism that can be leveled. . . is its lack of ultimate goals."[2] If the individual's experience is viewed as the measure of all things,

> One may well ask whether human experience is end enough in itself to justify educational effort. If we say that growth is an end in itself, we must ask, "growth toward what"? Surely growth implies direction-- human experience must be measured in terms of some goal. This lack of direction--this lack of goals beyond the problems of here and now--tends to rob man of his dignity.[3]

> Another criticism. . . is that it tends to produce people who are entirely self-centered in their outlook. Inasmuch as the individual's experience is raised to such a prominent position, we are likely to overlook the experiences of other people or of the group as a whole. An experience might be quite profitable to one individual but might prove harmful to those around him. It would not be difficult to imagine a situation in which the enrichment of one's own experience would in turn frustrate the personal growth of those around him.[4]

Of course there are those who would disagree with Venable's views of progressivism. Some would argue that he has defined it too narrowly, that individual experience is indeed related to group experience. (Essentialists and those of other persuasions may be taken to task for the same reasons.)

The reconstructionists may be criticized also on their pragmatic approach to knowledge, that it is only of value when it helps to solve problems. But the reconstructionists emphasize the solution of societal problems, not of individual problems per se.

Some of the questions asked of the existentialists' views on knowledge include: How can a society exist without a certain common knowledge which is taught to everyone? How can a society exist with everyone learning what he wants to learn, experiencing what he wants to experience? Isn't there a need for some commonality of knowledge? Some of the same questions raised of the progressivists are directed to the existentialists. What is the direction of existentialist education? Isn't direction important? How can one's scope of thinking be broadened if he only relies on his experience for learning?

What is subject matter for the adult learner is thus not an easy question to answer, but we leave it to go on to the next question: How should what is to be taught (the knowledge or subject matter) be determined?

There are at least three crucial dimensions to this question:

1. Who should determine the content?

2. What are the routes to determining the content?

3. What are the sources of subject matter ideas?

Figure 7 illustrates the major components of these three questions.

Who determined content	Routes	Sources of content ideas
The adult educator	Authoritarianism	Contemporary life
The learner	Empiricism	The individual life
The learner and the adult educator	Intuitionism	Subject matter discipline
	Rationalism	

Figure 7

Who should determine the content? Should the adult educator, by himself, determine what should be taught? The adult educator can study contemporary life, he can study potential adult learners, and he can look to the subject-matter disciplines for sources of content ideas. Tyler[5] suggests a study of contemporary life can include such categories as health, family, recreation, vocation, religion, consumption, and also the economic, social, and political situation.

A study of the potential learners can reveal such things as the needs that people have, a comparison of the present condition of the learners with some desirable standard of what should be.

The discipline can be studied to determine what facts, concepts, and theories it contains.

Following through with the example of the adult educator determining the content, the next problem with which he is faced is what route to follow in choosing content from the three sources--contemporary life, study of the individual, and the discipline.

Royce[6] discussed four routes for determining knowledge-.-authoritarianism, empiricism, intuitionism, and rationalism. The adult educator who accepts the authoritarianism route will accept what authorities say about contemporary life, the potential learners, and the discipline. The adult educator who follows the empiricism route will not accept ideas from any of these three sources until he has had an opportunity to test the ideas and verify them.

The adult educator following the intuitionism route will select knowledge based on his intuition--what seems right for him to select. For example, his intuition may tell him that all adults should know something about the workings of government so they can live successfully in a democratic society.

Following the rationalism approach, the adult educator, using logical thought, will reach decisions about what should be taught from the ideas he has gotten through study of contemporary life, study of the individual, and study of the discipline.

Often there will be a combination of routes used. The adult educator may start with intuitionism, what he thinks might be appropriate knowledge. He may check his hunch with an authority; he may also check it empirically with, for example, an advisory group of potential learners. He may also spend considerable time thinking logically about all the ideas he has before making a final decision about which knowledge he will select to be taught.

This same process may be used by the learner ascertaining for himself what knowledge he wants. And it may likewise be used by a combination of learners and adult educators in determining what should be taught.

But the same basic issue remains: who should decide what the content should be--the adult educator, the learner, or some combination of learner and adult educator? And does it make a difference if the content is seen as having value for its own sake, something that everyone should have, or seen as having value only so far as it can contribute to individual or societal problems? Under what conditions might the learner determine what the content should be? Under what conditions should the adult educator make that decision? And under what conditions is it appropriate for some combination of learner and adult educator to determine content together?

FOOTNOTES

1. Tom C. Venable, Philosophical Foundations of the Curriculum (Chicago: Rand McNally, 1967), p. 53.

2. Ibid., p. 52.

3. Ibid., p. 55.

4. Ibid.

5. Ralph W. Tyler, Basic Principles of Curriculum and Instruction (Chicago: University of Chicago Press, 1950).

6. Joseph R. Royce, The Encapsulated Man (Princeton, N.J.: D. Van Nostrand Company, Inc., 1964).

BELIEFS ABOUT THE LEARNING PROCESS

Two broad areas of concern will be discussed in this section: instructional objectives and the learning process itself. A number of issues and concerns will be identified within each broad area.

Instructional Objectives

Most educators agree that instructional objectives are an important part of the learning process. It is argued that they can help the learning process in at least two ways:

1. They can serve as a guide for organizing action and direct the design of learning experiences.

2. They can serve as a basis for determining results of the learning activity, comparing what happened with what was planned.

There are many issues related to instructional objectives. For purposes of this discussion, instructional objectives are those associated with specific learning experiences or activities. They are different from, but obviously related to, the overall purpose of adult education. Instructional objectives should contribute to the broader purposes of adult education.

Issue 1: Should instructional objectives have a fixed quality? Or should they be flexible and subject to constant revision?

This issue is similar to the one discussed earlier about the essential nature of knowledge--certain knowledge that everyone should have versus knowledge that is tentative, of value only when it contributes to the solution of a problem, for example.

If certain knowledge has an essentialistic quality, then it follows that objectives related to this knowledge should also have a fixed quality. If knowledge is seen as tentative, then the instructional objectives are seen as tentative.

Issue 2: Should the objectives arise out of the learner's experience or should they be developed external to the learner's experience?

The essentialists would argue for the latter position, the progressivists for the former. The essentialists assert that the learner's experiences change too much, thus there is no constancy to what is taught. To get constancy, the instructional objectives must be developed external to the learner's experience.

Those taking the opposite view contend:

Aims (here defined to mean the same as objectives). . . must be tailor made for the occasion; we cannot publish a list of them in advance. We do not know our aims till

a situation arises and we project aims as a means of
guiding our observation and final selection of a plan
for handling it.[1]

Issue 3: Should or should not objectives be written in behavioral
terms?

This has been, and continues as a hot issue among professional
educators. Each side of the question has its followers who fill professional journals with articles denouncing the opposing position and
proclaiming the virtues of their position.[2]

Behavioral objectives generally have three components:

1. An indication of the content to be learned.

2. Observable behavior expected at the end of the learning activity.

3. A standard of performance below which the learner's perfor-
    mance is unacceptable.

Those who subscribe to behavioral objectives argue that we can only
determine if learning has occurred if we are able to observe a change
in the learner's behavior. And further, unless we know specifically what
we want to accomplish in a learning activity, it's impossible to know how
to implement the activity.

The opponents of behavioral objectives contend that following the
behavioral objective route may eliminate any attention to instructional
objectives which cannot be easily stated in behavioral terms. Some even
argue that the assumed definition of learning which the behavioralists
adhere to--that learning is an observable change in behavior--is incorrect.
These opponents leave open the possibility that much learning which takes
place does not immediately result in observable behavioral change, indeed
in some instances may never result in observable behavioral change
that can be traced directly to the learning activity.

The second source of disagreement with behavioral objectives is the
difficulty of anticipating all the learning outcomes from a given learning
activity. Some critics go farther and ask if educators should even try
to anticipate all learning outcomes. Some of the unanticipated learning
outcomes, these critics say, may be more important than those that are
planned.

Another dimension of the quarrel is the desirability of flexibility
in instructional objectives. Once a learning activity begins, it may
become obvious that the focus of the activity should be changed and the
objectives modified. Indeed, the students may demand that a change be
made. This may mean abandoning some previously determined objectives,
modifying others, or adding new ones. If the teacher has to adhere to a
pre-planned set of behavioral objectives, these options are impossible.

A third argument against behavioral objectives is that certain subject
matter doesn't fit the behavioral change model. One example is the study

of poetry, where the emphasis is on the feelings created in each person as a result of the learning experience, at the same time that it is impossible to predict what these feelings ought to be. It is also difficult to observe a feeling, in a behavioral sense.

There are broader concerns too, particularly when we think about the adult learner. What right has one man to plan what the subsequent behavior of another man should be? Maslow wrote:

> Do we ourselves want to be predicted and predictable? Controlled and controllable ?. . . I will say that questions come up here and clamor for treatment which do have something to do with the subjective feeling of being free rather than determined, of choosing for one-self rather than being externally controlled, etc. In any case, I can certainly say that descriptively healthy human beings do not like to be controlled. They prefer to feel free and to be free.[3]

What role should the adult learner have in determining what behavior he expects learners to demonstrate as the result of a learning activity? And how does the adult educator relate to the learner's role in behavioral objective determination?

Can planned learning occur in adult education settings when there are no behavioral objectives? How directed or nondirected should the learning experiences for adults be? Are there conditions when learning should be more directed, should follow the behavioral change route? Are there other conditions when the nondirected approach is more appropriate? What are these conditions and how do we determine them?

Are some adult educators overreacting to behavioral objectives and to the more directed learning situations? Brubacher wrote:

> . . .much of the anxiety over too much determinism or mechanism in education is unwarranted. By and large, the teacher should welcome every device that the educational psychologist or educational sociologist offers as a means of more certainly controlling the outcomes of instruction. . . consequently computerized and programmed instruction, often feared as mechanizing education, should be viewed, not as threats. . . but rather as assets in more economically giving (the learner) the power to achieve his ultimate goals of autonomy.[4]

Brubacher closes his discussion of this issue with, "Inescapable as freedom may be, it must be recognized that too much of it and too soon may overwhelm the uninitiated and sometimes cause him to abandon freedom for the security of authority."[5]

But what about the more experienced adult learner? Do adult educators have some obligation to help him experience the joy of personal discovery, personal growth and development, the expression of his freedom to learn as an autonomous individual ?

The issue is obviously not so easy as taking sides either for or against directed learning and behavioral objectives. What are the inter-relationships ? Does it make sense to follow one approach at one time, the other approach another time, or at times mix directed and non-directed instruction ?

The Learning Process

What is learning ? And how can we as adult educators best assure that learning occurs ? Within adult education and indeed within all of education today, there is great controversy among educators concerning these two questions. Essentially there are three basic "camps":

1. Those who believe that learning is the training of the mind and the acquisition of basic truths (mental discipline).

2. Those who believe that learning is conditioning or reinforcement (S-R associationists).

3. Those who believe that learning is the development of insight (Gestalt-Field).

To understand more completely the assumptions behind each of these theories, we must look at what we believe about the nature of man and the purposes of education.

The Alternative Learning Theory diagram is a summary of each learning theory as it relates to the nature of man and purpose of education, plus the teaching method implied and the related philosophical position.

Many who subscribe to the mental discipline theory believe that man is a ". . . special, spiritual creation of God living in His universe and enjoying earthly tenure at His pleasure. . . "[6] The mind of man is thought of as the captain while the body of man is the ship--thus a dualistic viewpoint. The purpose of education is to first, develop ". . . the implicit Powers of reason that lie embedded in the mind and, second . . . (stock) . . . the mind with knowledge. "[7]

Knowledge is something absolute, never changing. This

> . . . kind of knowledge can be produced by the mind
> only, not by the senses, since it comes from reason,
> not from experience. These twin beliefs about the
> means and end of inquiry stand central in the traditional
> thesis of mental discipline. [8]

Robert Hutchins through his Great Books program is a contemporary advocate of the mental discipline approach. He says:

> Education deals with the development of the intellectual
> powers of men, . . . (but) we cannot talk about the

intellectual powers of men, though we talk about
training them, or amusing them, or adapting them, and
meeting their immediate needs, unless our philosophy in
general tells us that there is knowledge and that there
is a difference between true and false. We must believe,
too, that there are other means of obtaining knowledge
than scientific experimentation. . . (and) if we are to set
about developing the intellectual powers of men through
having them acquire knowledge of the most important
subjects, we have to begin with the proposition that experimentation and empirical data will be of only limited use to
us. . . [9]

Knowledge is thus seen as having intrinsic value--it is of value by
itself as contrasted with the progressivists who believe it must have
some instrumental value.

The S-R associationists suggest that man is ". . . purely a biological
creature, a complex nervous system lacking an inorganic mind and an
immortal soul, and living in a strictly materialistic universe. . . "[10]
Man is thus seen as a biological creature without a separate entity called
"mind."

Learning, then, becomes conditioning or reinforcement. There is
considerable diversity among those who broadly subscribe to the S-R
associationist theory of learning. Three representatives of the S-R associationist theory are Edwin Guthrie (Contiguous Conditioning), Clark
L. Hull (Deductive Behaviorism or Reinforcement Theory), and B.F.
Skinner (Operant Conditioning, Beyond Freedom and Dignity). [11]

The broad purpose of education is the transmitting of knowledge:

The ultimate goal of neobehaviorists (a term used to
describe modern day S-R Associationists) is to reduce
learning to physio-chemical factors. Learning consists
of impressions of new reaction patterns on a pliable,
passive organism. Since learning arises in some way
from an interplay of organisms and their environment,
key concepts of neobehaviorists are stimulus (that which
is provided by an environment) and response (that
reaction which is made or given by an organism). Con-
sequently, the problem of the nature of the learning
process centers in the relationships of respective sti-
muli and responses and what occurs between them. [12]

Those who subscribe to the Gestalt-Field theory of learning believe
that man is ". . . a biosocial animal living in a given natural world
through means of received but not unalterable social order, a world
in which all parts are inextricably related and of which he is an integral
part . . . "[13]

The Gestalt-Field advocates focus on the key word "insight" when

Table 2

Alternative Learning Theories

Learning Theory	Nature of Man	Purpose of Education	Method	Related Philosophy
Mental Discipline	Micro-Cosmic Mind Dualistic: Mind and Body Separate	Train the Intellect Pass on the Culture	Transfer of Knowledge Cultivate the Mind	Idealism: Essentialism Perennialism
S-R Associationism	A Sense Mechanism	Master Facts and Information	Conditioning and Reinforcement Focus on Parts	Realism: Essentialism Perennialism
Gestalt-Field	Experiencing Organism	Help People Cope with Environment. Help People Change Environment.	Problem-Solving Focus on Wholes	Progressivism Reconstructionism Existentialism (In some forms)

describing learning. Learning is seen as the process of

> . . . developing new insights or modifying old ones.
> Insights occur when an individual, in pursuing his
> purposes, sees new ways of utilizing elements of his
> environment, including his own bodily structure. The
> noun learning connotes the new insights--or meanings--
> which are acquired. The Gestalt-Field definition of
> insight is a sense of, or feeling for, pattern or relation-
> ships. To state it differently, insight is the 'sensed
> way through' or 'solution' of a problematic situation.
> Insights often first appear as vague 'hunches.'
> We might say that an insight is a kind of feel we get
> about a situation which permits us to continue actively
> serving our purposes, or trying to.[14]

To the Gestalt-Field advocates there may be learning without an
observable change in behavior. Experience is emphasized over behavior
with experience defined as ". . . an interactive event in which a person
comes to see and feel the consequences of a given course of action,
through acting and seeing what happens."[15]

What are the interrelationships among these three learning theories?
Is it possible for an adult educator to generally subscribe to Gestalt-
Field theory and yet, in specific learning situations, follow a mental
discipline or a S-R associationist approach? For instance, are there
contradictions if an adult educator claims to follow Gestalt-Field theory,
yet uses teaching machines in his instructional program?

FOOTNOTES

1.   John S. Brubacher, <u>Modern Philosophies of Education</u> (New York: McGraw-Hill Book Company, 1969), pp. 100-101.

2.   See Richard C. Anderson, ed., <u>Current Research on Education</u> (Englewood Cliffs, N.J.: Prentice-Hall, 1969), for an indepth discussion of this issue citing positions taken by McNeil, Mager, Atkin, and Popham.

3.   A.H. Maslow, <u>The Farther Reaches of Human Nature</u> (New York: The Viking Press, 1971), p. 14.

4.   Brubacher, <u>Modern Philosophies of Education</u>, p. 128.

5.   <u>Ibid.</u>

6.   Charles J. Brauner and Hobart W. Burns, <u>Problems in Education and Philosophy</u> (Englewood Cliffs, N.J.: Prentice-Hall, 1965), p. 18.

7.   <u>Ibid.</u>, p. 35.

8.   <u>Ibid.</u>

9.   Robert M. Hutchins, <u>The Conflict in Education in a Democratic Society</u> (New York: Harper and Row, 1953).

10. Brauner and Burns, <u>Problems in Education and Philosophy</u>, p. 18.

11. See Morris L. Bigge and Maurice C. Hunt, <u>Psychological Foundations of Education</u> (New York: Harper and Row, 1962), for a discussion of the differences among these three positions.

12. <u>Ibid.</u>, p. 292.

13. Brauner and Burns, <u>Problems in Education and Philosophy</u>, p. 18.

14. Bigge and Hunt, <u>Psychological Foundations of Education</u>, pp. 296–97.

15. <u>Ibid.</u>, p. 301.

SUMMARY

In previous chapters we have considered general and educational philosophies, several alternative beliefs about the adult learner, beliefs about the overall purpose of adult education, beliefs about content, and beliefs about the learning process.

Now, in summary fashion, I'll relate beliefs in the above areas to three broad, but alternative learning models: (1) learning as problem solving, (2) learning as acquiring content, and (3) learning as self-actualization. I am being quite arbitrary in selecting three models. Vandenburg,[1] for example, discusses eighteen different models.

The three models I've selected, as broad as they are, do relate to the three philosophical positions I've developed throughout this monograph:

Progressivism–Reconstructionism: Problem Solving

Essentialism–Perrenialism: Acquiring Content

Existentialism: Self–actualization

There are also dangers when we put beliefs into categories as I'm doing here. These three models are not entirely discrete and often meld together. For instance, at a given time an adult educator may focus on learning as problem solving, but at the same time the learner is usually acquiring content too. You can also argue that both the acquisition of content and the solving of problems should contribute to a person's self–actualization.

Others argue that the appropriate learning model depends on the learning situation. At times learning is problem solving, at other times it may be content acquisition, and still other times its focus is toward a person's self–actualization.

Most educators, though, lean toward a particular learning model. The following table illustrates beliefs about the function of content, the roles of the learner and the adult educator, the learning goals, and related learning theory for each model.

Problem Solving

Problem-solving learning focuses on the problem (s) of the learner, and/or the problem (s) of the learner's community or the larger society. The learner's personal problems may be primarily (1) economic in nature--how to increase income, (2) sociological--how to relate to one's neighbors, (3) psychological--how to cope with one's fears, (4) spiritual--how to relate to a higher being.

Societal problems may include the sum of the personal problems that people have in a given community. If everyone in a community has

Table 3

Learning Models

	Problem Solving	Acquiring Content	Self-Actualization
Function of Content	A Means	An End	A Means
Role of Learner	Problem Solver	Recipient of Content	Self Searching
Roles of Adult Educator	Helper, Knowledge source	Translator, Communication link, Advocate	Guide, Counselor
Learning Goal	Problem Solving	Mastery of Information and Facts	Finding One's Self
Related Philosophy	Progressivism Reconstructionism	Essentialism Perennialism	Existentialism
Related Learning Theory	Gestalt-Field	Mental Discipline Stimulus Response Gestalt-Field	Gestalt-Field

a relatively low income, that problem is both individual and communal.

But societal problems need not be the sum of individual problems. Inadequate cultural opportunities in a community may not be a personal problem for a large number of people living in a particular community. Yet without improved cultural opportunities the community may not be able to attract certain kinds of firms whose employees insist that cultural opportunities be available before they will relocate there. The problem is thus one which affects the entire community, though it may not affect each individual now living in that area.

The role of the adult educator in a problem-solving situation is to:

1. Help people with problem finding. Scheffler expresses the need for problem finding this way:

An education modeled in scientific thinking could not possibly remain content with the student's initial problems; it would seek to introduce him to new ones and train him to explore further for himself. More generally, it would strive to create wider perception as well as to improve problem-solving capacity, to develop an alertness to unsettled and conflicting elements in experience as well as a drive to organize, unify, and resolve.[2]

2. Help people learn the problem-solving process. One measure of the success of the adult educator is the extent to which the learner becomes comfortable enough with the process to be able to solve succeeding problems with little or no help from the adult educator. It's an error when the adult educator solves the problem for the learner. The learner, rather than becoming independent becomes more dependent. Because the adult educator has solved one problem for him, the learner will return again and again to the adult educator with problems to be solved.

3. Be a knowledge source or help find knowledge that may contribute to the solution of the person or the community's problem. In many instances the adult educator by virtue of his training and experience will have available the knowledge necessary for the solution of many problems. In other instances the adult educator will know someone else who has the necessary competence, or he will know where the knowledge is available in a research report, in a book, etc.

The learner's role in a problem-solving situation is threefold. He must become adept at problem finding, he must become knowledgeable about the problem-solving process, and thirdly, he must work toward the solution of his or the community's problem(s).

New knowledge is acquired by the learner through the process of problem solving, so there is obviously a relationship between the problem-solving process and the content acquisition. Problems cannot be solved, in most instances, without the learner acquiring content. But knowledge may be acquired without any problem being solved. Indeed, some knowledge acquisition situations may lead to finding new problems for the learner.

Acquiring Content

Broudy says, ". . . while an Experimentalist or Instrumentalist (problem solving) theory of knowing accents the learner's efforts to predict what will extricate him from some predicament, a Realist account (acquiring content) of the matter will stress the attainment of accurate concepts and precise relationships among them. In summary, Realistic methodology (acquiring content) can be expected to be interested in perceptual reorganization, concept attainment, abstraction, and insight as basic to the learning process. "[3]

One example of how some adult educators have emphasized acquiring content is the practice adoption model.[4] Following this model, the adult educator assumes that some content (research results, new ideas, etc.) should be obtained by the learner. The model includes the following steps: (1) awareness, (2) interest, (3) evaluation, (4) trial, and (5) adoption.

The adult educator presents the content, following the practice adoption stages, with the hope that the learner will learn (adopt) the new ideas, research result, etc. In some instances the adult educator will translate content so it is more easily understood by those not familiar, for example, with research jargon. The adult educator can also be a communication link from the sources of ideas to the learners. In some situations the adult educator may be the advocate of certain knowledge that he, and others, believe certain learners should have.

For example, until the 1940's farmers planted open pollinated field corn which yielded, under the best conditions, less than fifty bushels per acre. Researchers discovered that by planting hybrid field corn, the yield per acre could be doubled. But the farmers needed to know that hybrid corn existed, and that they could increase their yields by planting it. Cooperative Extension Agents throughout the corn planting regions of the country followed the practice adoption model in helping farmers learn about and plant hybrid corn. They advocated certain knowledge they felt farmers should have.

Self-Actualization

Learning for self-actualization focuses on the individual learner and his situation. Fallico says, "The mission of the teacher ends with his efforts to help another human to want desperately to be himself, at all costs and risks. "[5] The problem for the teacher, according to

Fallico, is,

> How can we guide humans to choose to become self-
> determining agents in their thinking and in their
> valuing without asking them to give up the privacy
> of their own self-birth into being? The position of
> this problem is predicated on the simple proposition
> that a world of men self-alienated lies in no world at
> all, however much convention, science, religion, or
> smooth diplomacy may succeed in holding the sorry
> mess together. There is no substitute for self-search
> in the education of man. And no man can help another
> in these fundamental matters except by denying him
> palliatives and expedient ways of avoiding the genuine
> encounter with nothingness which is existence itself. [6]

What is the adult educator's role then, if he subscribes to self-actualization for the learner? Maslow talks about a Taoistic relationship:

> Taoistic means asking rather than telling. It
> means nonintruding, noncontrolling. It stresses
> noninterfering observation rather than a controlling
> manipulation. It is receptive and passive rather
> than active and forceful. [7]

Carl Rogers says it this way, ". . .it is the quality of the personal
encounter which matters most. . . the quality of the personal encounter
is probably, in the long run, the element which determines the extent
to which this is an experience which relates or promotes development
and growth.[8]

Content serves as a means toward self-actualization. The learner's
role is to discover himself, in relation to his situation. "The teacher
is under moral responsibility to guard against the invasion of a man's
anguished search after himself."[9]

Discussion

There are many learning models. In this chapter I've suggested
three: learning as problem solving, which focuses on the problems of
learners and/or their communities; learning as acquiring content, which
focuses on content; and learning as self-actualization which focuses on
the learner and his situation.

There are several questions we could raise related to these three
learning models.

Is it possible to believe that the overall purpose for learning is to
lead toward the self-actualization of individuals, and that both problem
solving and content acquisition can contribute to this broader purpose?

Are there situations when it is absolutely essential that learners
get certain content, e.g. preparing persons to become medical doctors?

Assuming such situations exist, can such acquiring of content also contribute to that person's self-actualization? Are there certain teaching strategies and techniques which preclude self-actualization ever occurring? Will certain learners achieve self-actualization, solve their problems, or acquire content, in spite of the learning model the adult educator follows? For instance, is it possible for a learner to work toward self-actualization as he works with programmed learning activities? Is it possible for a learner to solve his problems when an educator focuses on the dispersal of subject matter?

FOOTNOTES

1. Donald Vandenberg, ed., Teaching and Learning (Urbana, Illinois: University of Illinois Press, 1969).

2. Israel Scheffler, in Martin Levit, ed., Curriculum: Readings in the Philosophy of Education (Urbana, Illinois: University of Illinois Press), p. 115.

3. Harry S. Broudy, "Learning as Acquiring," in Teaching and Learning, ed. by Donald Vandenberg (Urbana, Illinois: University of Illinois Press, 1969), p. 52.

4. Lincoln David Kelsey and Cannon Chiles Hearne, Cooperative Extension Work, 3rd ed. (Ithaca, N.Y.: Comstock Publishing Associates, 1963), pp. 266-69.

5. Arturo B. Fallico, "Existentialism and Education," in Nature, Aims, and Policy, ed. by Adrian Dupuis (Urbana, Illinois: University of Illinois Press), p. 169.

6. Ibid., p. 170.

7. A.H. Maslow, The Farther Reaches of Human Nature (New York: The Viking Press, 1971), p. 15.

8. Carl Rogers and Louis N. Nelson, The Nature of Teaching (Waltham, Massachusetts: Blaisdell Publishing Company, 1969), p. 297.

9. Fallico, "Existentialism and Education," p. 164.

Chapter 10

CLOSING COMMENTS

Development of a working philosophy of adult education is more than an intellectual exercise. It is not so simple as reading, reflecting on what you've read--and then you have a philosophy. Action is an essential part of the process.

Reflection $\rightleftharpoons$ Action

Reflection by itself does not lead to the development of a working philosophy of adult education, nor does action by itself. Action means to try out your beliefs. Discuss them with other people. Put them to work as you participate in seminars, lead discussions, attend planning meetings, organize resources, develop teaching materials, and do all the other things adult educators do. A working philosophy is developed by action, and then reflecting on the activity. We reflect and act, we act and reflect; we always do both. Through this process we constantly refine our working philosophies.

In the beginning, if you haven't already thought much about your working philosophy, you may spend considerable time reflecting. But the next stage, acting on your reflections must follow.

Throughout these pages I have constantly raised questions, occasionally providing alternative answers to them. Following are a few of my beliefs--where I stand on some of the issues. I will quickly relate that my personal working philssophy in not complete, but is in the process of becoming. There are segments of it that trouble me and cause me to do much reading, much reflection, and much trying out of my beliefs in real life situations. I don't apologize for these tactics. To me this is a part of the process of refining a working philosophy. I'm concerned about the person who tells me he has figured out his working philosophy and is finished with it, once and for all, to be used by him for the rest of his life. I want to leave my philosophy open, subject to new reflections and action.

I am constantly working toward consistency in my beliefs. It's often argued that we must accept inconsistency. The argument goes somewhat as follows: Because there is so much inconsistency in the actions of people and institutions, because there are so many contradictions, it is impossible to have a consistent system of beliefs, indeed it may even be inappropriate.

I argue that a person who believes that inconsistency in beliefs is the answer has temporarily stopped in his search for consistency. Recognition of inconsistency is one place along the road to consistency. It is a temporary resting place, not an appropriate stopping place.

Another issue relates to the purpose of adult education. Should adult education work toward the improvement of society, or should adult education strive to help people improve themselves? Are we more interested in people or are we more interested in societies?

I am interested in both people and societies. Through the process of solving societal problems, people can grow and develop. Through the process of personal growth and development, societies can improve. For me it is not an either-or issue, but a both-at-the-same-time issue.

One of the major issues of the day for many educators is the Gestalt-Field approach to learning vs. the behaviorist approach. Though I have tried to show both sides of that issue in this monograph, it's evident that I favor the Gestalt-Field side of the question. I firmly believe in the integrity of the individual learner. I do not believe that an educator has the right to manipulate another person, to determine what his behavior should be.

I cannot accept the position that man is essentially a biological creature quite similar to other animals. I believe man has a mind and soul. I also believe that man is constantly searching to understand himself, how he relates to his natural and social environment, and how he relates to a Higher Being. For me, learning is a process by which man actively seeks these understandings. A person may learn by reflecting on his own ideas without any planned input of content, by solving personal and social problems, by acquiring new information, by participating in planned behavioral change situations. A person may learn without displaying change in behavior, but often a changed behavior is a natural outcome of learning.

I believe my role as an adult educator is primarily a helping role, not an interfering role. I believe a person should be what he is to be, not what I, or an institution, believes he should be.

APPENDIX

Following is an example of how the author used the material in this monograph in a graduate seminar. The seminar approach is obviously but one of many approaches that may be used. The overall purpose of the seminar was for each participant to write his personal working philosophy of adult education and share it with fellow students.

The seminar included fifteen graduate students who were either completing master's degree programs in Extension or adult education, or were well along in doctorate graduate programs in these same areas. Eight of the seminar participants were international students from Africa, Europe, the Middle and Far East, Canada, and South America. Seven were U.S. students from throughout the country. Ages ranged from thirty to thirty-five. All of the students had adult education experience, some as professors of adult education, some as community development leaders, several as extension professionals, and one as a staff member working with cooperatives and credit unions.

A variety of opportunities were offered seminar participants, including:

1. Individual reading.

2. Organizing sharing experiences.

3. Writing tentative position papers.

4. Sharing position papers with other students.

5. Completing a paper on their working philosophy.

The materials in this publication and a reading list, which included the books I have listed at the end of each chapter, were distributed to all students. Early in the semester some readings were suggested as beginning places for students. But beyond these early suggestions, students were encouraged to read what they wished. They were encouraged to go beyond the reading list if they discovered an area of interest they wanted to explore more deeply. One student read considerably in the area of existentialism. Another got interested in Fromm and Maslow and read well beyond the reading list.

Throughout the semester small groups of students (3-4 per group) organized each week's sharing experiences. The seminar outline provided at the beginning of the semester was used by the students as a framework for organizing these experiences. The seminar outline included four main areas:

1. Getting acquainted with the concept of working philosophy.

2. Looking at general and educational philosophies.

3. Reviewing the issues within each of the suggested working

philosophy framework areas.

4. Sharing working philosophies.

When students got to the part of the seminar that dealt with issues within each of these suggested framework areas (the learner, the overall purpose of adult education, etc.), they were encouraged to write their beliefs in each of these areas. The issues were discussed each week in class and the instructor reacted, in writing, to each tentative position paper.

Toward the end of the semester students were invited to share their working philosophy papers with the entire seminar. These presentations evoked a great deal of discussion and interest.

The broad framework for the seminar included reading, personal introspection, interaction with students and professors, and writing. These activities did not occur in stepwise fashion, however. After interacting in class there was more introspection and considerable re-writing of positions.

Excerpts from Students' Papers

Following are excerpts from papers written by students in the seminar to provide some of the flavor of how they dealt with the issues.

Beliefs About the Adult Learner

Man is a unique being. Maslow states that "each person's inner nature is in part unique to himself and in part species-wide." The "species-wide" or "common denominator" inner nature of man can be easily discerned, but it is the wise and sensitive individual (e. g. the educator) who can tap the unique nature of each man and help each to realize this within himself and help it to grow.

Man is ultimately a selfish being. His motivation basically is based on self-interest even though some of his behavior may appear to be selfless. Whatever man does, for whatever reasons he chooses to elucidate, he does it out of personal need or want or desire. For example, even altruistic behavior, though selfless in appearance, is selfish. Ask a philanthropist why he does good for others, the answer will probably be because he likes to help others. Press further and ask why he likes to help others, and he likely will say because it makes him feel good, because it gives him satisfaction to see others happy, etc. Man is what he is and he does what he does for himself.

Man ultimately stands alone. This refers to the basic difference between loneliness and aloneness. Man can avoid or overcome loneliness; man cannot avoid aloneness; he must come to terms with it and thus gain strength from it.

Man's innate predisposition is neutral. Man is neither good nor bad.

If man's nature is encouraged, nurtured, guided, positively reinforced, it can be good; if it is denied and suppressed, it can be evil. Life and circumstance will determine each man's basic nature and accordingly help it to develop and/or change.

Man has great potential to grow. A Peanuts cartoon once depicted Linus bearing "the burdens of potential." It is a burden only if it is not tapped. Each man is capable of much greater growth than he even begins to accomplish in one lifetime. Man must come to terms not only with his actuality, but he must realize his potentiality. Man must integrate what he is and what he can become.

Man is born free and autonomous. Socialization processes more often than not kill or at least dull this freedom and autonomy. Educators should help individuals restore and/or retain the freedom to be themselves.

Man is a total being of mind and body mutually interacting. However, man must deal with his basic bodily needs before he can begin to deal with the affective and cognitive realm of his being. Once the basics are satisfied and man has reached higher mental development, then the possibility of mind over matter comes into existence, i.e. bodily needs no longer are prevalent nor do they require much attention--witness mystics and those involved in meditation and higher consciousness levels. Thus, the interaction of mind and body can move through several levels where at one level the body predominates in the interaction, at another level there develops an equilibrium state of interaction, and where at still another level the mind is dominant in this interaction. Using an analogy found in one of the handouts where the mind of man is likened to a captain of a ship and the body of man is likened to the ship itself, I see the role of the captain being that of navigating and guiding the ship. Such a role is functional only when the ship has been attended to and it is in good shape and in good working order. And so, the mind dictates to the body only after the bodily basic needs have been attended to and have been satisfied.

Man is a part of nature. Nature is a natural, physical given. Although man is an integral part of nature, he is distinct from it because he has a mind, he has a "soul," he has a "consciousness about his life." As the mind and body interact, so too man and nature mutually interact and move through varying levels of interaction. Man at one stage of his development was dominated by nature; as man developed, the interaction with nature became more equal until man's present stage of development where he has learned to dominate and influence his relationship with nature. However, evidence shows that man has influenced nature to the point of destruction. Man can and should control his environment, be it nature or societal forces or both. But, he now must learn to convert his interacting influence on nature to a positive, non-destructive force, mutually beneficial to both.

Man is master of his fate and thus is responsible for his actions. Maslow states "man has his fate within him, dynamically active at this present moment." He is the result of all his experiences over which he can have control. I think one of the basic goals of life should be working toward increasing control over that life, meaning his own, not that of others.

Man is a social being. This is not contradictory with the above statements about man's selfishness or his aloneness or his freedom and autonomy. Man cannot exist without other men. If he does, then it becomes a question of the length of such an existence and the quality of this existence. Man needs man.

In short, man is many things. He is a unique and selfish being. He is a totality of mind and body, a neutrality of good and bad. He stands alone yet is a part of nature and his society. He is a free and autonomous being who can control his fate and master the forces which buffet him. However, in spite of all this, man does not even come close to realizing, understanding, accepting and utilizing the potential, the greatness within him. He settles for far less. The role of an educator can so easily be defined--to help man realize that which he is capable of becoming, of being; to help him, if he should want help, to grow, to learn to become; and, to help him realize that with such movement in him, society will improve and grow also. Society is simply that collectivity of learning individuals. Man owes it to himself and to his society to grow and to become all that he can and wants to become. Danger looms when man gets so caught up in social causes, societal change and improvement that he forgets and ignores himself in the process. I would even speculate that if man's first concern was knowledge of the inner self, its growth and development, then societal change and betterment would come more easily, more readily, and more effectively. Man needs to be self-directed before he can become other-directed. It has been said that man needs to love himself before he can begin to love others. So too when man knows himself can he begin to know and to understand others as individuals and as collectivities. However, it has also been said that man can know himself only by being other-directed. I can accept that when I envision man's self-knowledge occurring at certain kinds of levels. For example, man first must begin with himself, he must begin self-knowledge with and by himself. Once the process has begun, then he moves outward, he becomes other-directed and thus begins to move to another level of self-knowledge. After a point, he must again look inward, he must again become inner-directed, then outer-directed, and so on and so forth. Each level increases his self-knowledge, each level moves him toward self-actualization.[1]

---

[1]Written by Vida Stanius

The Purpose of Adult Education

In examining the purpose of adult education, I find a division into short-term and long-range goals is helpful. The adult educator must have immediate goals in mind when he sets the stage for learning. These goals should be designed to help the learner identify and satisfy his immediate felt needs. These needs may cover a wide spectrum, from learning a new skill in order to facilitate job advancement to filling a desire for intellectual stimulation or an even deeper search for love or excitement.

No matter what the adult educator's short-term goals are they should be designed to facilitate his long-range goals. For me, this long-range goal is to help each individual reach his human potential. By this I mean that each person should strive to throw off the negative aspects of his personality such as fear, deceit, suspicion, narrow mindedness and hatred and let his human potential for love, hope, and understanding develop. Fromm describes these favorable characteristics as "humane experiences" which he says are attainable only by transcending the ego. I believe that every individual is born with great potential for goodness and that adverse characteristics have developed in us because of undesirable environmental influences. These environmental influences have led most of us astray in our search for happiness and self-fulfillment.

A major obstacle I see in reaching our human potential is an over-dependence on outside authority for answers to our problems. Since the time of the cave man when people relied on various gods for security from the unknowns of thunder, storms, and eclipses, we looked to more powerful outside authority for answers. Today many of us still rely almost totally on the church or government for security. We are afraid of change because that destroys our security which depends on maintaining the status quo. We are capable of loving only those things which are close and familiar to us. We cannot attain deep joy or fulfillment because of an underlying fear of losing our security.

An important role of adult education, it seems to me, is to help individuals develop more security in themselves and their fellow man while depending less and less on outside authority. This will lead to better understanding of self and others, openness, an inquiring mind, and eventually to trust. The unknown will become a challenge rather than something fearful. People of different cultures and/or values will be viewed as sources of new knowledge and understanding rather than something only to guard against. The development of understanding and trust, first in ourselves, then in others, can best be reached through relating to others in what Freire calls "dialogue." Self-fulfillment or movement toward human potential through dialogue can lead to a true love for mankind. This "love" is not necessarily an agreement with others' beliefs and values but an acceptance of them as human beings and an understanding of their human potential for goodness. This process, in which dialogue can play an active part, is what I understand Maslow to be referring to when he talks about self-actualization.

I believe in Freire's theory that individuals working and striving
to expand their vision in dialogue with others will eventually lead to
societal reform. Reform is not the ultimate goal but a consequence of
the ultimate goal which is to make learners aware of themselves as
human beings and to contantly   explore and strive to understand the world
around them.[2]

---

[2]Written by Ronald M. Jimmerson